THE
KINDERGARTEN PHASE
OF ETERNITY

YAKIMA BIBLE BAPTIST CHURCH
6201 TIETON DRIVE
YAKIMA, WA. 98908
509-966-1912

By

Dr. James Wilkins

New Testament Ministries
Dr. James Wilkins
1700 Beaver Creek Dr.
Powell, TN 37849
817-909-8010
865-938-8182
pwilkins96@sbcglobal.net

DEDICATION

Dedicated to the 65 million Americans who are over 55 years old and have passed into the second semester of the kindergarten phase of their lives.

INTRODUCTION

Kindergarten Principles That Will Transform ADULTS

STOP!

GO NO FURTHER IN THIS BOOK!!

If you are to understand and do well in your Kindergarten course, you must read this Introduction.

WELCOME TO OUR CLASS

Welcome to our course on *The Kindergarten Phase of Eternity*. Just as a child enters Kindergarten and then proceeds through the 1st, 2nd, 3rd grades, etc., until they finish college, one continues to learn even after graduation from this life, through death. In fact, one's education begins to accelerate at that point.

In comparison to the thousand-year time segment of the millennium and on into the endless ages of eternity, one's uncertain lifespan of 70 – 85 years on earth is very brief indeed.

In our study, we refer to one's entire lifetime on earth as **the Kindergarten phase of life**. It is imperative for us to understand that our life now (Kindergarten phase) is the time for us to prepare for the millennium (1000-year reign on earth), and the eternal ages to come.

SOME ARE ALREADY IN THE SECOND SEMESTER

It is obvious that some of our generation, because of their advanced age, are in the second semester of the Kindergarten phase of life. Others are nearing graduation. Their natural lives are almost over. They have accepted their role of finding whatever happiness they can while they live out the rest of their existence on earth. They have given up any hope of making any significant contribution to mankind and are basically marking time.

Your teacher wants to especially encourage these second semester students to take this course and study with renewed hope.

"IT AIN'T OVER 'TIL IT'S OVER"

Abraham (age 100) and Sarah, his wife (age 90), would have missed the whole purpose of their lives and would have died failures, if they had retired at age 75. John the Baptist, a man who powerfully influenced the world, was born of aged parents who were beyond the age of childbearing. It took a miracle of God to bring it to pass; and God, who is not a respecter of persons, still performs miracles today. Caleb, at age 80, became one of Israel's greatest generals and heroes.

vi

History reveals that 64% of the greatest accomplishments on earth have been achieved by people who have passed their 60th birthday. One famous major league baseball manager had a saying, "It ain't over 'til it's over." That is certainly true concerning your life.

TEACH US TO NUMBER OUR DAYS

If this short life span is the Kindergarten phase of our life, and its purpose is to prepare us to live in the millennium, then it is time to become serious about this course.

In Psalms, chapter 90, God revealed to David the briefness of the Kindergarten phase of our life. He said,

> *A thousand years is like yesterday when it is past. A thousand years is like a watch (3 hours) in the night. Life is like last night's sleep that is over. Life is like an on-rushing tsunami, which is traveling hundreds of miles an hour. Life is like a story that has been told. Life is like the grass which has died and turned brown.*
>
> *After hearing about the briefness of time, David cried out, "Teach us to number our days, that we may apply our hearts unto wisdom." (Psalm 90:12)*

THE BEST WAY TO STUDY AND REMEMBER

There are only six short lessons in this course. For the best results, the author suggests that you take a full week for each lesson. Begin on Monday by reading the whole week's lesson. When you have finished reading, answer the questions for Monday. Turn back and look up the answers and fill in each blank. Do your Daily Declaration and begin learning that week's memory verse.

On Tuesday, review Monday's answers before re-reading the lesson and completing Tuesday's work. By reviewing your answers for each daily exercise before going to the next section, a person's retention rate increases, on an average, to 62%.

Read the lesson once and you will soon forget most of these eternal truths. Read the lesson and then review it on a daily basis for one week, and you will never forget these vital principles, which will help you graduate with honors.

A FINAL WORD FROM YOUR TEACHER

The laws of big numbers, which the insurance companies use to determine the cost of insuring people's lives, say that the average man my age will live for 82.4 years. At the age of 74, provided the Lord doesn't come first, your teacher has about 8 years to live before graduation (death).

After graduation, your teacher will take a short vacation in Heaven before going to the Judgment Seat of Christ, where the deeds done in the Kindergarten phase of his life will be judged. After this

Judgment, I will be assigned a place of service on this earth for 1000 years. These 1000 years could be a time of joy, happiness and honor, depending upon the lessons learned in the **Kindergarten phase of my life**. It also could be 1000 years of pain and regrets.

It is obvious that my work for the Lord is not over yet because I am still alive. I have not graduated yet. The same is also true for you, because you are still alive.

MY QUESTION TO YOU

If where I live, and the position I fill, during the millennium depends on what I do in the Kindergarten phase of my life, which time segment should I be more concerned with? The eight years before I graduate, or the 1000 years where I will serve after graduation?

The obvious answer is for me to accept God's grace to finish Kindergarten with honors during my final eight years, so I can hear His, "Well done, my little Kindergarten child," when I stand before Him at the Judgment Seat. Since I only have a short time, I should use it wisely to fulfill my purpose on earth so I will have a place of honor for the entire 1000 years in His glorious Kingdom.

MY CHALLENGE TO YOU

Come on students, let's enter into our studies so you can finish Kindergarten with assurance and honors. Our goal for you is to have a good report card at the time of your graduation.

TABLE OF CONTENTS

LESSON ONE

Thou art worthy, O Lord, to receive glory and honour and power: for thou hast created all things, and for thy pleasure they are and were created. (Revelations 4:11)

LESSON ONE
Kindergarten Is Important

God the Father spoke of His love for man in John 3:16,

> *For God so loved the world, that he gave his only begotten Son, that whosoever believeth in him should not perish, but have everlasting life.*

There are at least four important truths presented in this verse:

1.   The fact of God's love for all men

2.   The sacrificial death of Jesus

3.   The place of faith in salvation

4.   The concern that God has for man is for his eternal good

The principle upon which we would like to elaborate is the loving God, concerned for man's eternal good. This is only natural since the eternal God created man in His image and likeness.

A loving, domestic father is concerned for his son when he goes to Kindergarten. In Kindergarten, the little boy is to learn phonics, how to read, and develop his skills under discipline. If the son does well in Kindergarten, it will greatly shape the rest of his life. But as important as Kindergarten is, it is only a very small part of the son's overall education and development.

Our lifetime of possibly seventy to eighty years on this earth is very much like Kindergarten, in comparison to the 1000-year millennial reign and the eternal ages that stretch out before the child of God and constitute his life.

Kindergarten is compared to our lifetime on this earth. It is short and comes to an end. Just as Kindergarten ushers in other important periods of one's life, so does the end of this life. Death, for the child of God, is not the end but only the glorious beginning. He crosses over and begins a short vacation in Heaven before receiving his stewardship for his 1000 years of further service on this earth.

KINDERGARTEN CAN BE A HINDRANCE

Kindergarten can be a hindrance to a child when the parents do not use the opportunity wisely.

- They use Kindergarten just as a babysitting facility.

- They allow their child to be self-centered and undisciplined.

- They do not aid their child in mastering his phonics.

16

- They have no time to help their child with his reading.

At the end of the child's Kindergarten year, he is undisciplined, self-centered, unprepared for further training, and confused about what his role in life is all about.

> The natural life of 70 – 80 years is the Kindergarten phase of our life.

He is well on his way to a diminished life, instead of a life of success and happiness. The parents and the child did not realize the purpose of Kindergarten. As a result, the child will suffer the consequences forever.

THE WAY ONE LIVES HIS LIFE CAN BE A HINDRANCE

Just as a bad Kindergarten experience can be a great hindrance to a child, a misspent 70 – 80 years on this earth can greatly hinder the child of God in his position in the millennial and the eternal realm of his life.

Think of life as three-dimensional:

Dimension One: Kindergarten – natural life of possibly 70 to 80 years.

Dimension Two: The 1000-year millennial reign on this earth under King Jesus.

Dimension Three: The eternal ages, which stretches out into the infinite forever.

The natural life of 70 – 80 years is the Kindergarten phase of our life.

The 1000 years on this earth will be determined by how well we do in Kindergarten.

The Kindergarten phase of our life will also decide the degree of glory we will share in the eternal ages to come.

A WRONG CONCEPT OF LIFE AND TIME

Many of God's children have a false concept of life. They believe that the child of God, when he dies, goes directly into the eternal Heaven and remains there forever. They have not understood that there is a Judgment Seat, where they will have to give account of their stewardship while on earth. Their works will be tried by fire before going into the period of 1000 years, called the millennium. This period will be followed by the Great White Throne of Judgment. Then God will make a new Heaven and a new earth and usher in the eternal ages.

> Death is only a servant to deliver the child of God safely and instantly into Heaven.

To be absent from the body means that in an instant the child of God will be present with God in Heaven (2 Corinthians 5:8). With one tick of the clock, he will be on earth. With the next tick, he will be in Heaven. Death is only a servant to deliver the child of God safely and instantly into Heaven. But as glorious as this truth is, it does not contradict or change the fact that there will be a Judgment Seat, followed by 1000 years on this earth before entering into the new

Heaven and the new earth where we will live forever.

A better concept of what happens when a child of God goes to Heaven is one who goes on a splendid vacation. He rests from his labors before going back to the earth and a place of service during the 1000-year reign, and then on to the eternal ages. Words cannot describe the importance of the Kindergarten phase of our life on the earth. Our Heavenly Father longs for His children to understand their purpose and then apply themselves properly to fulfilling it. So much hangs in the balance!

Much of people's thinking about eternal things and what happens when one dies is based on the sentimental philosophy of the make-believe world...

KINDERGARTEN QUESTIONS THAT PRODUCE RIGHT CONCLUSIONS

Much of people's thinking about eternal things and what happens when one dies is based on the sentimental philosophy of the make-believe world, and not on the eternal Word of God. In order to clarify and establish proper thinking, we will offer some questions designed to establish clear thinking.

QUESTION ONE: How much coaching of your mother and father did you have to make in order to persuade them to conceive you?

QUESTION TWO: How many reminders did you have to send to your mother, while she was carrying you, in order to ensure that you would be born a normal, healthy baby?

QUESTION THREE: How much effort did you have to make when you entered into the process of your human birth?

The answer to all three of these unusual Kindergarten questions is: NONE. Then the question arises, "Who gave you life?"

QUESTION FOUR: What advance courses did you complete in a previous world in order to be able to regulate the exact chemical make-up of your body so you would have a sound mind? Or was there someone else who created such a marvelous body for you to inhabit and enjoy?

> How many thousands of electronic devices do you have alerting you of the many dangers that constantly surround you? Or is there someone who protects you and preserves your life?

QUESTION FIVE: How much planning did it take for you to program your heart to beat 100,000 times each and every day of your life? Or did someone else supply you with that marvelous organ?

QUESTION SIX: How many thousands of electronic devices do you have alerting you of the many dangers that constantly surround you? Or is there someone who protects you and preserves your life?

If you didn't have anything to do with giving yourself life; if you didn't have anything to do with designing and programming your body, then who did?

Someone gave you the mind that enabled you to learn millions of bits of information and data, which you have used in accumulating and maintaining your livelihood.

Someone gave you life.
Someone gave you a body.
Someone energized your life day by day.

When you stop and think about how little you had to do with where you were born and what you would look like, then the questions arise, "Why was I born? Why am I alive? What is my purpose on earth?"

If you had so little to do with obtaining such a magnificent body, and the computer-like brain and the eyes that have the ability to recognize, compute and send messages to the nervous system without one even knowing about it, then the questions arise:

"Can I continue to live as if I am in charge, or should I seek to find out who created me and why? **Shouldn't my position be one of stewardship, rather than ownership?"**

"If someone else made this awesome body and gave me so many natural abilities through a sound mind, good eyesight and coordination, then to what extent and purpose were my talents to be used?"

In the make-believe world, where many fantasies arise, there are myths, fables and much confusion about pre-existent life, this life, and after-life. But the eternal Word of God is very clear. Man is the only being God created who will live forever.

SIMPLE ANSWERS TO KINDERGARTEN QUESTIONS

There are simple and direct answers to the Kindergarten questions in God's eternal Word.

- First, God gives life.

That was the true Light, which lighteth every man that cometh into the world. (John 1:9)

The Bible clearly teaches that God lighted, or gave life, to every person when He came into this world.

- Second, God maintains life.

> *Thou art worthy, O Lord, to receive glory and honour and power: for thou hast created all things, and for thy pleasure they are and were created.*
> (Revelations 4:11)

The apostle Paul clearly answered the question about who maintains a person's life in the sermon on Mars Hill. He said,

For in him (Jesus) *we live, and move, and have our being.* (Acts 17:28)

- Third, God made you for His pleasure.

After the rapture (the second coming of Jesus for His saints), the 24 leaders or elders in Heaven will be worshipping our Redeemer. Their words clearly state that all things were created for the pleasure of God.

Thou art worthy, O Lord, to receive glory and honour and power: for thou hast created all things, and for thy pleasure they are and were created. (Revelations 4:11)

● Fourth, God is the owner.

In the light that God created man for His pleasure and that God gives man life when He comes into his life, then it is not surprising that the Bible clearly announces that man belongs to God. Paul seemed a little surprised that men do not recognize the owner-ship of God when he asked, "What? Know ye not that your body is the temple of the Holy Ghost which is in you, which ye have of God, and ye are not your own?" Then he gave the answer of who man belongs to when he continued,

> *For ye are bought with a price: therefore glori-fy God in your body, and in your spirit, which are God's.* (1 Corinthians 6:19-20)

MAN'S POSITION IS ONE OF STEWARDSHIP, NOT OWNERSHIP

In our Kindergarten class, we have seen the answers to our questions with the obvious conclu-sions. Man is not his own because God created him and gave him life. God gave him the ability to think every thought and perform every movement. There-fore, man's position as a creative being is not one of ownership, but stewardship. Paul scolded the Corinthians after he asked,

> *For who maketh thee to differ from another? and what hast thou that thou didst not receive? now if thou didst receive it, why dost thou glory, as if thou hadst not received it?* (1 Corinthians 4:7)

23

The early church members were acting like they were better than others. So, Paul asked them some questions that caused them to think and act properly. Kindergarten kids of all ages have had the same problems. It was hard for them to accept their proper role of stewardship, instead of one of ownership.

Man is an eternal being, and as an eternal being, God has a purpose for man on this earth, which will benefit man eternally. This life is to be similar to the Kindergarten year. Just as Kindergarten is not the main show, this life is only a small, though important, part of man's life on this earth.

God, who gives man certain talents that are to be used to honor and glorify God, brings man to this earth. If man learns the purpose of the Kindergarten phase of his life and submits to it, then he will bring tremendous glory to God during the Kindergarten period. God will then elevate him to a place of royalty during the 1000-year reign on this earth. God's will is to make us *"kings and priests"* and for us to give glory to God during the 1000-year Kingdom on this earth. (Revelations 1:6)

> Man is an eternal being, and as an eternal being, God has a purpose for man on this earth, which will benefit man eternally.

24

THE DANGER OF NOT LEARNING KINDERGARTEN SKILLS

If a person does not learn that his role on this earth is one of stewardship and not ownership, he will not complete the Kindergarten phase of his life properly. This will greatly affect where he lives and what he possesses in the 1000-year reign. There is the possibility that he could lose everything but his soul.

IMPORTANT QUESTIONS FOR A KINDERGARTEN KID TO THINK ABOUT

1. What do you have that the world says is legally yours?

2. Where did you get it?

3. What are you doing with it?

4. Is God getting any glory from it?

5. In the light of what you are doing with what God has given you, should God give you any more?

THE REST OF THE BOOK

If there have been challenging questions and thoughts in this first chapter, then some of the lessons on the following pages will be life-changing. ***The Kindergarten Phase of Eternity*** is so important to learn about. Ask God to help you for proper discernment and understanding. In succeeding lessons, you will learn that God's greatest desire is to develop His Kindergarten kids **so they can share in His eternal glory**.

POINTS TO PONDER

● God's love for man, and Jesus' sacrificial death, was for man's eternal good.

● The Kindergarten phase of our life is compared to our lifetime on this earth.

● The three dimensions of life are:

  1. Kindergarten phase of possibly 70 to 80 years.

  2. The 1000-year millennial reign.

  3. The eternal ages, which stretch into the infinite.

● Man's position as a created being is **not one of ownership**, but one of stewardship.

● The danger for one who does not learn good Kindergarten skills – may cost him everything except his soul.

● God's greatest desire is to develop His Kindergarten kids **so they can share in His eternal glory.**

LESSON ONE QUESTIONS
Kindergarten Is Important

MONDAY – KINDERGARTEN IS IMPORTANT

1. The _____ that God has for man is for his _____ good.

2. Kindergarten is only a _____ small part of our _____ education and development.

3. Kindergarten is like our _____ on this earth.

4. Kindergarten can be a _____ to a child when the _____ do not use the opportunity _____.

TUESDAY – THE WAY ONE LIVES HIS LIFE

1. A _____ 70-80 years on this earth can greatly _____ the child of God in the _____ and _____ realm of his life.

2. The _____ life is possibly 70-80 years.

3. They believe that the child of God, when he dies, goes _____ into the eternal Heaven and remains there _____ .

4. With _____ tick of the clock, he will be on _____. The next _____, he will be in _____ .

5. He _____ from his labors before going back to the earth and a place of _____ during the _____ reign, and then on to the _____ ages.

WEDNESDAY – QUESTIONS THAT PRODUCE RIGHT CONCLUSIONS

1. Much of people's _____ about eternal things and what happens when _____ dies is based on sentimental _____ .

2. Then the _____ arises, "Who gave _____ life?"

3. Was there someone else that _____ such a _____ body for you to _____ and enjoy?

4. Shouldn't my _____ be one of _____ instead of ownership?

5. If someone else made this awesome body, then to _____ extent and _____ were my _____ to be used?

THURSDAY – SIMPLE ANSWERS TO KINDERGARTEN QUESTIONS

1. *"That was the true light which _____ every_____ that cometh into the world."* (John 1:9)

2. *"For In him (_____) we _____, and move, and have our _____."* (Acts 17:18)

3. *"For thou hast _____ all things, and for thy _____ they are and were _____."* (Revelations 4:11)

4. Paul seemed a little _____ that men do not _____ the ownership of God.

5. *"Therefore glorify God in your _____, and in your _____, which are _____."*

FRIDAY – MAN'S POSITION IS ONE OF STEWARDSHIP

1. Man is _____ his _____ because God _____ him and gave him _____.

2. Therefore, man's position as a _____ being is not _____ of _____, but stewardship.

3. God will then _____ him to a place of _____during the _____ reign on this earth.

4. What do you _____ that the world says is _____ yours?

5. God's greatest _____ is to develop His Kindergarten kids so they can _____ in His eternal _____.

29

DAILY DECLARATION

Repeat aloud each morning and evening:

"I will humble myself as a little child, so I can finish my life in victory."

MEMORY VERSE

The earth is the Lord's, and the fullness thereof; the world, and they that dwell therein.
(Psalm 24:1)

CHECK BLOCK AFTER REPEATING

	Mon.	Tues.	Wed.	Thurs	Fri.	Sat.	Sun.
A.M.							
P.M.							

I now dedicate my life to be a faithful steward over the things God has placed in my hands.

Signature

_____

LESSON TWO

And be not conformed to this world: but be ye transformed by the renewing of your mind, that ye may prove what is that good, and acceptable, and perfect, will of God. (Romans 12:2)

LESSON TWO
The Development of Talent in Kindergarten

A good Kindergarten teaches its students about God and His love. That is what this phase of our eternal life is for, to learn about God and His love.

A good Kindergarten has structured lesson plans with stated objectives. In this section, you will find that God has a structured plan with stated objectives for you in *the Kindergarten Phase of Eternity*.

A good Kindergarten begins to teach simple, logical points. Very shortly, you will see God's simple logic for your life and learn about the kind of attitude God will bless.

A good Kindergarten depends on its students to make good individual decisions. You will see that God gives each person the right of choice; to do good, or to do evil. Paul gave the foundation for these truths in the following verses:

> *I beseech you therefore, brethren, by the mercies of God, that ye present your bodies a living*

sacrifice, holy, acceptable unto God, which is your reasonable service. And be not conformed to this world: but be ye transformed by the renewing of your mind, that ye may prove what is that good, and acceptable, and perfect, will of God. For I say, through the grace given unto me, to every man that is among you, not to think of himself more highly than he ought to think. (Romans 12:1-3)

THE KINDERGARTEN CLASS LEARNS ABOUT GOD'S LOVE

This is the first thing a little child should be taught. God loves you. The proper definition of the word "history" is HIS STORY. Everything begins with God, is about God, reveals God, and is for God's glory. Earlier, we discovered that God gives life. He *"lighteth every man that cometh into the world."* (John 1:9)

We have seen that *"in him we live, and move, and have our being."* (Acts 17:28)

We have learned that we are not our own because:

- God gives us life;

- God continues our life; and

- God redeemed us back to Himself by giving His life.

These principles were the truths Paul taught to the Roman church in his letter. (Romans 11:33-36) Please remember that the book of Romans was first written on a scroll, and was not divided into chapters and verses until many years later. Chapter 11, verse 36 and chapter 12, verse 1 were not divided.

Paul summarized his teaching in verse 36:

● That everything was of God.

● That everything was through God.

● That everything was to God.

● That everything was for God's glory.

Then, Paul concluded talking about God's power, His wisdom, His love for man and His glory, by writing, "I beseech you therefore," or "because of this." When one sees the word "therefore" in the Scripture, he should pause and find out what it is "there for." Paul said, I beseech you, or beg you, therefore, (or because of these marvelous truths: everything was of God, through God, to God and for God's glory) to do something.

The primary reason God created this vast universe was to demonstrate His wisdom, glory and power. David declared this truth when he wrote, *"The heavens declare the glory of God."* (Psalm 19:1)

One of the main reasons Jesus came to the earth and became flesh is so we could better see God's glory, love and grace. (John 1:14)

It is almost beyond man's ability to think that this infinite God made us in His image and likeness, and created everything in this beautiful world for us and our eternal pleasure. (Ephesians 2:7)

I beseech you, or beg you, therefore (or because of these marvelous truths: everything was of God, through God, to God and for God's glory) THAT YOU DO SOMETHING. That something is that we are to learn how to please God and share in His eternal glory.

THE KINDERGARTEN CLASS REVEALS LESSON PLANS

Much of the training that a dedicated Kindergarten teacher receives has to do with lesson plans, which are designed to produce the right discipline and objective in the life of the students. Our Creator, who gave us life, is our all-wise and loving teacher and has a perfect plan for each of our lives.

Jesus announced the plan. In John 10:10, Jesus stated that the devil came to be the destroyer of men's lives. He destroys man every way he possibly can. He steals affection away from parents and family and causes heartache and confusion in every home. He steals opportunities away in order to make life seem hopeless. The devil is the master of deception and thievery, and constantly wars to distract from God's plan for your life.

The devil is also a killer. Not only does he bring physical death to people, but he is the killer of love, a killer of dreams, and a destroyer of hope. Jesus described the devil's final work as one of destruction and confusion.

In this world of hurt and harm, where mankind is dying, Jesus stated His lesson plans for man. He said, *"I am come that they might have life."* John 10:10 The life that He was referring to is eternal life, which comes through the new birth.

36

The new birth, or becoming a Christian, is not the climax to the purpose for which Jesus came into the world. No, it is the very first lesson that God wants one to learn in our Kindergarten phase of life.

Jesus went on to state, in that same verse, *"That they might have life, and that they might have it more abundantly."*

He not only came to this earth that we might have life, but that we might be victorious in our life. His desire is not for one to become a victim, but to

It is almost beyond man's ability to think that this infinite God made us in His image and likeness, and created everything in this beautiful world for us and our eternal pleasure. (Ephesians 2:7)

become the victor. He designed life so that man can become a champion and overcome and master all facets of life.

Paul commented on these plans. In Romans 12:2, Paul described the lesson plans and objectives for the Christian life as, *"that good, and acceptable, and perfect, will of God."*

Just as God made every snowflake different from any other snowflake;

Just as He made every leaf on every tree different from any other leaf;

Just as He made every thumbprint or DNA different from everyone else;

God has created you to be unique, different from

any other human on this earth; and **He has designed a good, and acceptable, and perfect will for you to find and master**. Remember, *the Kindergarten Phase of Eternity* was designed for your future glory and happiness in the coming phases of your life. Paul also stated that the child of God is saved by grace *"unto good works, which God hath before ordained that we should walk in them."* (Ephesians 2:8-10)

STOP and think!

The troubles you encounter and overcome by the grace of God in your Kindergarten phase of life are designed for your eternal glory.

This infinite God, Who created this vast universe and then gave His Son to die on Calvary's cruel cross, has marked out a life for you that is a good and acceptable life to you. In fact, Paul even went further in his description of God's lesson plans and objectives for you, and described them as a perfect plan!

Peter summarized the process God uses to reach this perfect, eternal plan. This loving God, your Teacher, longs for the very best for each of His Kindergarten kids. In the final chapter of the first book of Peter, God summarized His objectives for our lives. Note the objective – **eternal glory** – and the steps outlined to obtain it:

1. *"But the God of **all grace**,"*

2. *"who hath **called us**"*

3. *"unto **his eternal glory** by Christ Jesus,"*

4. *"after that ye have **suffered a while**,"*

5. *"make you **perfect** (mature), **stablish, strengthen, settle you**."* 1 Peter 5:10

The troubles you encounter and overcome by the grace of God in your Kindergarten phase of life are designed for your eternal glory. The Apostle Paul stated that,

For our light affliction, which is but for a moment (in comparison to eternity), *worketh for us* (the people who go through it) *a far more exceeding and eternal weight of glory.* (2 Corinthians 4:17)

The life He has given us in our Kindergarten phase WILL DICTATE HOW we will share in His future glory.

THE KINDERGARTEN CLASS REVEALS LOGICAL PROCEDURES AND ATTITUDES

Paul also gave the proper attitude one should have in the light of these two great truths. These truths, once again, are:

1. God gave us life and placed us on earth for a "good, acceptable, and perfect" purpose.

2. The life He has given us in our Kindergarten phase WILL DICTATE HOW we will share in His future glory.

In the light of these truths, there are two logical questions that arise:

1. What type of service does God require of His children in order to share in His future glory?

2. What should the attitude of His children be in their service to Him now?

He taught that the child of God has a higher standard than the standards of this world, a God-like, or holy, standard.

THE REASONABLE SERVICE TO GOD

In the light of these two great truths, Paul listed a lifestyle that he called a "reasonable service."

First, he said a reasonable service is to present your body as a living sacrifice to follow and do God's will. Jesus explained to the apostles what presenting your body as a living sacrifice meant when He admonished them to *"Seek first the Kingdom of God and His righteousness"* and *"follow me."*

Second, Paul said to present our bodies as a holy, living sacrifice. Again, Jesus taught that the believer is in the world, but not of the world. He taught that the child of God has a higher standard than the standards of this world, a God-like, or holy standard.

Third, he said our service should be acceptable unto God. Paul admonished the young pastor, Timothy, to *"study to show himself approved unto God, a workman."* (2 Timothy 2:15) He also stated in 1 Thessalonians 2:4 that he sought to please God and not man.

Fourth, Paul strongly stated that the believer should *"be not conformed to this world."* One may ask, "What does 'be not conformed to this world' mean, and how can one not be conformed to this world?" Be not conformed means – do not live like those

The Bible is God's perfect Book, which He placed on this earth to serve as a manual for His children.

who live in the lost worldly system live. Do not accept their standards of what is "cool" or "hip." Do not accept what the world system says is proper behavior.

In answer to the questions of "How can we not be conformed to this world?" Paul gives the solution. One should be transformed, by the renewing of his mind, to what the acceptable standards are that are pleasing to God.

What does renewing your mind mean and how can one do it? The Bible is God's perfect Book, which He placed on this earth to serve as a manual for His children. In this manual, God reveals conduct that He is highly pleased with. Other people did things that God was very displeased with and, He showed His displeasure toward them.

One renews his mind by reading the Bible and following the standard of conduct that is pleasing to God. Paul told Timothy to study, or be diligent in learning, the right procedures of pleasing God.

He told him to,

Be thou an example of the believers, in word, in conversation, in charity (love), in spirit, in

*faith, in purity. Till I come, give attendance
to reading, to exhortation, to doctrine.*
(1 Timothy 4:12-13)

Peter taught his converts that the way to please
God was through a process of adding to their personal faith in Christ.

Peter's list of principles of spiritual growth are
found in 2 Peter 1:5-7. He said,

> *Add to your faith, **virtue** (good habits); and to
> virtue, **knowledge** (Bible knowledge); and to
> knowledge, **temperance** (self-control); and to
> temperance, patience; and to patience, **godli-
> ness** (God-like-ness); and to godliness, **brother-
> ly kindness**; and to brotherly kindness, **chari-
> ty** (love). (2 Peter 1:5-7)*

As one obeys in adding these attributes to his life,
he becomes closer to God, which produces greater joy
and happiness. He grows into a mature, strong Christian.

THE KINDERGARTEN CLASS TEACHES ITS STUDENTS TO MAKE GOOD DECISIONS

The great God of Heaven lays out all the facts and
then humbly allows His children to make their own
decisions. He works in their lives to teach them to
have proper attitudes in the Kindergarten phase of
life, but He does not force them to do so. Each person
is free to make his own choice.

The proper attitude of the child of God is this light,
that God has given us everything:

- Our life

- Our talents

- Our thoughts, energy and movement

Then what should our attitude be toward Him?

It should be a humble attitude. Paul said, *"Through the grace given unto me,"* one should not *"think of himself more highly than he ought to think."* (Romans 12:3) God does give us our lives. He offers us wisdom. He offers us grace. He gives us favor and works within us. Because this is true, we should walk humbly before Him and be grateful for the wonderful things He does through and with us each day.

When one has a humble, submissive attitude, then God has a free hand to help and bless His child.

It should be a submissive attitude. Paul admonished us to,

> *Present your bodies a living sacrifice, holy, acceptable unto God, which is your reasonable service.* (Romans 12:1)

This request, present yourself, shows that the child of God has a choice of what he will do. He can submit himself unto God, or he can do his own thing.

God's desire is to make your life one that is "good, acceptable, and perfect." On the condition that one humbly submits to God's manual and leading, He will exalt him to share in His eternal glory. So, the prop-

43

er attitude we should have is one of humility and sub-mission. When one has a humble, submissive atti-tude, then God has a free hand to help and bless His child.

It should be a vigilant attitude. Paul started out dealing with the proper attitude by saying, "I beseech you." Literally, I beg you, to present your bodies. Why did Paul start with those words, "I beseech you"? Paul knew that man has a strong will, and oftentimes a rebellious spirit. Our old human nature does not like to be told what to do. We have a tendency to rebel sometimes, even when we know that what we are told to do is right and that it is for our benefit and good. Because of our nature, Paul approached this sensitive subject by saying, "I beseech, or beg, you to present your bodies."

> So the child of God should be vig-ilant in watching for this self-suffi-cient attitude.

We also have another tendency. After we learn and, in our minds, master a certain truth, the human nature gets very self-sufficient. We think we can do it on our own and begin to walk in our own strength. This is the reason Paul admonished, in verse three, for people not to think of themselves more highly than they ought to think.

So the child of God should be vigilant in watching for this self-sufficient attitude, and realize that it is pleasing to God for us to humble ourselves and sub-mit to the teachings of the Bible.

It is logical and manifests a right attitude when we present our bodies a living sacrifice, holy, acceptable unto God, which is our reasonable service. Then our loving Father can reveal that good, acceptable and perfect plan that He has for our life. WHAT A DEAL! We submit and follow the leading of our loving Father through the Kindergarten phase of our life, which climaxes with Him sharing His eternal glory with us forever.

POINTS TO PONDER

- Kindergarten kids must learn that we are not our own:
    God gives us life.
    God continues our life.
    God redeemed us back by giving His life.

- God has a good, acceptable and perfect plan for our lives.

- God created everything for us and **our eternal pleasure**.

- Man has a choice either to **submit to God's plan**, or do his own thing.

- Paul begs man to make the right decision and present his body a living sacrifice.

- If we submit to God's leading in Kindergarten, it will benefit us forever.

- God's desire is for us to share in His eternal glory forever.

LESSON TWO QUESTIONS

The Development of Talent in Kindergarten

MONDAY – THE DEVELOPMENT OF TALENT

1. You will find that God has a _____ plan with stated _____ for you in the Kindergarten _____ of your life.

2. Everything begins with _____, is about _____, reveals _____, and is for _____ glory.

3. _____ redeemed us back to _____ by giving His _____.

4. This _____ God made us in His _____ and likeness, and _____everything in this beautiful _____ for us and for our _____ pleasure.

5. You should do something. That _____ that is that we are to learn how to _____ God and _____ in His eternal glory.

47

TUESDAY – THE KINDERGARTEN CLASS REVEALS LESSON PLANS

1. The _____ is the master of _____ and_____.

2. In this world of _____ and _____, where mankind is _____, Jesus stated His _____ _____ for man.

3. He not only _____ to this earth that we might have _____, but that we might be _____ in our life.

4. Paul described the lesson plans and objectives for the _____ life as, "that _____, and _____, and _____ will of God." (Romans 12:12)

5. The Kindergarten phase of your _____ was designed for your future _____ and _____ in the coming phases of your life.

WEDNESDAY – PETER SUMMARIZES THE PROCESS

1. This _____ God, your _____, longs for the very best for each of His _____ kids.

2. Note the objective – _____ glory.

3. The _____ you _____ and _____ by the grace of God in your Kindergarten phase of life are _____ for your eternal _____.

4. Our _____ affliction is but for a _____ in comparison to _____.

THURSDAY – THE REASONABLE SERVICE TO GOD

1. Present your _____ as a living sacrifice to _____ and ____ God's will.

2. Jesus taught that the believer is ____ the world, but not ____ the world.

3. "_____ to show yourself _____ unto God."

4. Do _____ accept what the _____ system says is proper behavior.

5. One ____ his mind by reading the _____ and _____ the standard of conduct that is _____ to God.

6. As one _____ in adding these _____ to his life, he becomes _____ to God, which produces greater _____ and happiness.

FRIDAY – THE KINDERGARTEN CLASS TEACHES TO MAKE GOOD DECISIONS

1. God humbly _____ His children to make their _____ decisions.

2. One should _____ "think of himself more highly than he _____ to think." Romans 12:3

3. He can _____ himself unto God, or he can do his own _____.

4. When one has a _____, ____ attitude, then God has a _____ hand to help and ____ His children.

5. The child of God should develop a _____ attitude of _____ for this _____ attitude.

49

DAILY DECLARATION

Repeat aloud each morning and evening:

"I will strive to be humble, submissive and vigilant as I journey through the Kindergarten phase of my life."

MEMORY VERSE

I beseech you therefore, brethren, by the mercies of God, that ye present your bodies a living sacrifice, holy, acceptable unto God, which is your reasonable service. (Romans 12:1)

CHECK BLOCK AFTER REPEATING

	Mon.	Tues.	Wed.	Thurs	Fri.	Sat.	Sun.
A.M.							
P.M.							

Realizing that I am not my own, but have been bought by the precious blood of Jesus, I will therefore strive to work for God and be faithful in my service regardless of personal sacrifice.

Signature

_____

LESSON THREE

But none of these things move me, neither count I my life dear unto myself, so that I might finish my course with joy, and the ministry, which I have received of the Lord Jesus, to testify to the gospel of the grace of God. (Acts 20:24)

LESSON THREE

The Place To Prepare For Living Is Kindergarten

My dear friend, Dr. H.B. Hubbard, at the age of 88 stated, "It is a tragedy that most **people** live all their lives before they **discover** what life is all about."

My comment concerning his statement is, **"His generation was smarter** than our present day generation. Most of **our generation will have to die** before they discover what life is all about."

This makes this section doubly important. Study carefully the information we will share with you. **Your eternal status may depend on it**.

WHAT WE HAVE LEARNED

FIRST: God's purpose for you on this earth is good. There is a good, acceptable and perfect plan for you, which, if followed, will give you an abundant and victorious life.

All things work together for good to them that love God, to them who are called according to his purpose. (Romans 8:28)

SECOND: God's purpose is for your eternal good. This Kindergarten phase may have some difficult lessons for you to learn. As **you** journey through **Kindergarten**, there may be some **struggles**, dark **days** and setbacks. There may be some times when you do not feel "the greatest," and you may get on a slippery slope where you take two steps forward and slide back one. But God has promised that those difficulties, when submitted to, will lead you to a place where you will share in His eternal glory. Those difficulties were designed for your eternal good.

THIRD: God has an ordained way. You were saved by grace unto good works, which God has outlined for you to walk in.

> One of the greatest truths, which is almost hidden from this generation's view, is that God longs for your personal, daily fellowship.

"For as the heavens are higher than the earth," God's ways are higher than man's ways. But God will always give you the grace to follow. (Isaiah 55:8-9)

FOURTH: God has a personal plan for your life. One of the greatest truths, which is almost hidden from this generation's view, is that God longs for your personal, daily fellowship. He wants to help you in the smallest matters in your life. One of the greatest pictures in the Bible is God as your papa – your daddy. You are His little boy or girl and there is nothing too small for Him to care about and render direction and help. The

54

Bible says He is touched by your feelings and smallest hurts.

WE CAN LEARN FROM OTHERS

Perhaps the greatest way Kindergarten kids **learn** is **by the observation of others**. A small child learns what he can get by with by watching what his older brothers and sisters get by with. The strongest teaching a younger child can have is from the good role models of his older siblings.

The Bible contains many stories of people who were saved and found God's purpose for their lives on earth. By submitting to God's will and purpose, they grew spiritually and became heroes and champions among their contemporaries. A study of their testimonies will shed light on the purpose of life for those living in our generation.

WE CAN LEARN FROM A MISSIONARY

When one who is familiar with the Bible thinks about a missionary, his mind goes directly to **the Apostle Paul**. One of the most thrilling parts of the New Testament is the record of Paul's missionary journeys.

Paul's most vivid memory – Paul told of his conversion from Judaism to Christianity in several places, which indicates that he spoke of it often. It was **vivid** in his memory. Listen as we take the words from Paul's own lips as he spoke of his divine purpose on this earth. Paul was quoting Jesus as he stood in King Agrippa's courtroom while on trial for

55

his life. *"But rise, and stand upon thy feet: for I have appeared unto thee **for this purpose***" – to get people saved and then train them so they can join in the effort of getting other people saved. You can read the entire quote concerning Paul's purpose in Acts 26:16-18.

Paul's greatest concern – Paul had spent 30 years in his pursuit of getting people saved by the time he visited some of the churches he had started years before. As he ministered to them, they all tried to persuade Paul not to go to Jerusalem because of the physical dangers that he would incur there, and probably even his death. Paul answered them by saying,

> *What mean ye to weep and to break mine heart? for I am ready not to be bound only, but also to die at Jerusalem for the name of the Lord Jesus.* (Acts 21:13)

> *Neither count I my life dear unto myself, so that I might finish my course* (purpose) *with joy.* (Acts 20:24)

Paul's greatest joy – During the days before his execution in the city of Rome, he wrote, *"I have finished my course* (purpose)." (2 Timothy 4:7) Then he left this world with a shout as he went to become a partaker of Christ's eternal glory. Listen to the great anticipation Paul had just before his execution,

> *Henceforth there is laid up for me a crown of righteousness, which the Lord, the righteous judge, shall give me at that day.* (2 Timothy 4:8)

WE CAN LEARN FROM A FAILURE

When you learn the name of this particular failure, you will be shocked! In the opinion of history and of the world, this man, a King, with his vast fortune, power and influence was a tremendous success.

In the light of examining his accomplishments in this short Kindergarten journey, Solomon did accomplish a great deal. But when you examine his life **in the light of God's purpose for his life**, particularly in the light of the eternal ages to come, **Solomon was a failure!**

The order of importance with which Solomon viewed his life is found in Ecclesiastes 1:1. His greatest calling was that **of a preacher.** To Solomon, his second most endearing position of importance was being **the son** of a famous and beloved king of Israel, King David. The third most important position was that of **King of Israel**. Although he led his nation to the highest state of power and glory in the history of Israel, he died a premature death **at the age of 59 in total disgrace**.

God gave Solomon one of the most important tasks that He ever gave to any man in Ecclesiastes 1:13. His job was to find out, by experiment, and record his findings on the subject,

> *What is man's purpose on the earth?* (Ecclesiastes 2:3)

God equipped Solomon with **a brilliant mind.**

He made him **an absolute monarch** where, as King, he answered to no man.

He gave him untold millions of dollars to conduct his experiment and **find out what the purpose for man's journey was through the Kindergarten phase of life on this earth**. After countless experiments, Solomon penned,

> *"Let us hear **the conclusion** of the whole matter (experiment): Fear God, and keep his commandments: for this is the whole duty of man. For God shall bring every work into judgment, with every secret thing, whether it be good, or whether it be evil.* (Ecclesiastes 12:13-14)

†

The cause of his failure was that he lived his life on the earth as if it were all there was to life.

One particular word – As a young man, Solomon was a **tremendous preacher**. He followed closely in his father's steps, but he had a short-term Kindergarten view of life. When he finished building the temple, his life lost its meaning and he went downhill from there.

But there is one short statement from Solomon's experiment concerning man's primary purpose on this earth **that should scream out** from the pages of divine writings. That statement was written by a man who, in the light of eternity, will be judged a failure. The cause of his failure was that **he lived his life on the earth as if it were all there was to life**. But this man, who failed to live his life in the light of eternity, was used of God to write words that have changed the lives of millions of people and gave them their real purpose for living. Solomon's famous words about life's purpose are,

> *The **fruit** of the righteous is a tree of life; and **he that winneth souls is wise**.* (Proverbs 11:30)

Man's primary purpose on this earth is to win souls.

WE CAN LEARN FROM A VISIONARY

There is perhaps no man in all of the Old Testament who was a greater visionary than Daniel. As a young man, this slave purposed in his heart not to compromise God's standards and defile himself. (Daniel 1:8) Even with threats to his life, he never detoured from his dedication to God. God revealed to him events that would take centuries to fulfill. God allowed Daniel to see the coming four major, worldwide powers, who have all come and gone. Daniel also foresaw the ancient revival of the old Roman Empire, which is taking place right before our generation's eyes.

Then it would not be surprising to learn that God also revealed to Daniel those who will be superstars under King Jesus during the 1000-year Messianic Kingdom on this earth.

Daniel revealed that the ones who have won many souls to Christ will be the ones who will shine the brightest during that time.

Daniel foretold that,

> *They that be **wise** shall shine as the brightness of the firmament; and they that turn many to*

59

*righteousness **as the stars for ever and ever**.* (Daniel 12:3)

We learn about man's purpose on this earth from the missionary who **went night and day after souls**. (Acts 20:31)

We learn from the man who was commissioned to find out man's purpose on this earth. Solomon said,

> The students in Kindergarten who learn and are wise will win souls.

He that winneth souls is wise. (Proverbs 11:30)

We learn from a man whom God allowed to look into the future to see who were the superstars during the coming 1000-year reign and find his report, "**The wise are as shining stars**."

What is the conclusion of man's primary purpose on earth? The students in Kindergarten who learn and are wise will win souls. To the members in our Kindergarten class who have not seen this truth, take courage. Before our Kindergarten course is over, we will reveal to you how you can also fulfill your purpose on earth and win souls. As your Kindergarten teacher, let me reassure you and give you my personal promise. **You can and**, if you follow our directions, **you will be part of winning someone to Christ**.

WE MUST LEARN FROM JESUS

Jesus was called the "Word of God."

60

In the beginning was the Word, and the Word was with God, and the Word was God. (John 1:1)

In verse 14 it states, "And the Word was made flesh, and dwelt among us."

Why was Jesus called "the Word"? Have you ever thought about that? What are words used to do? Words are used to communicate inward truth and feelings to those who cannot see the heart.

Jesus, as "the Word," was sent to the earth to communicate the heart and love of God. When we see Jesus and His life, works, miracles and tears, we are looking **into the heart of God**. So when we learn **why** Jesus came to earth and what is **important** to Him, we also **see** what is **important** to Almighty God.

FIRST: Jesus came to seek sinners. Jesus announced that His primary purpose on the earth was to seek and save sinners. His very words are recorded in Luke 19:10, *"For the Son of man is come to seek and to save that which was lost."*

SECOND: Jesus came seeking sinners in His daily life. There is evidence to believe that Jesus saved sinners **every day** in person-to-person conversations where He dealt individually with them. But, due to limited space in the Bible, only a few of those accounts are recorded in the Scriptures. These were recorded to send **a special message to the world**.

He walked miles to win a fallen woman. In John 4:4, it is recorded that Jesus *"needs go through Samaria."* Why? It was miles out of the way and would mean a very hot, strenuous journey.

61

The reason? There was a woman of a despised race who had been married five times, but was now living with a man who was not her husband. She needed to be saved.

What a message this soul-winning visit sends **to thousands of fallen women** who are living in shame! The message? "God loves you and will save you if you will let Him."

> There must be more to religion than just complying with commandments and observing empty rituals.

The little crook up a tree got saved. Zacchaeus was a crook, and a dirty publican who was part of a group very similar to the mafia today. Most people would have been afraid to talk to him about spiritual things. What a message this soul-winning message sends. **God loves the worst of sinful men**.

The head of the Synagogue got saved. Nicodemus, a master of Israel and in charge of a Synagogue, came to Jesus by night. His religion was not satisfying his empty heart. There must be more to religion than just complying with commandments and observing empty rituals. Jesus took time and gave the message that has been echoed around the world. In order to **go to Heaven, you must experience an inward change**. *"You must be born again,"* born from above.

What a message this one soul-winning visit sends. If you are going to Heaven, you need more than religion. You must become a new creature through a new birth.

Jesus saved the hopeless. In Mark, chapter 5, we have the account of a crazy man, who was possessed by demons, being saved. In verse 3, it is stated that **no man could tame him**. He was hopeless! Jesus and the disciples rowed across the sea, won the man, and left him *"sitting, and clothed, and in his right mind."* (Mark 5:15) This new convert wanted to get in the boat and follow Jesus, but Jesus commissioned him (as He does to all who are saved) to,

> Go **home** to thy friends, and tell them how great things the Lord hath done for **thee**, and hath had compassion on thee. (Mark 5:19)

What a message this one soul-winning visit sends. **After you are saved, you are to go and tell others about Jesus**.

There are other very prominent experiences where Jesus won people in His personal work, but these four **examples** are enough to show that Jesus, our **example, came seeking sinners**.

THE CHURCH'S PRIMARY JOB IS TO SEEK SINNERS

There are five accounts of the commission that Jesus gave to His Church. All of them make it clear that the primary purpose of the Christian Church is to get the Gospel to the lost. Mark's account stated,

> Go ye into **all** the world, and **preach** the gospel to **every** creature. (Mark 16:15)

63

John's account was,

*As my **Father** hath sent **me**, even so send I
you*. (John 20:21)

Many people who go to church regularly just go
and attend, never realizing that they, as a member of
the church, are to strive to win the lost.

WE MUST LEARN FROM JESUS' EMERGENCY

Today there is a special plea from Jesus to our 11th
hour generation. **Six billion souls** are out in the
Lord's vineyard, and most of them are **perishing**.
They are still lost and face the blackness and darkness, lost without God – **and time is running out**.

Six billion is more than all of the previous generations **combined**! Most of them are lost!

Can you visualize how this awesome reality must
affect our Heavenly Father, whose only desire is to
love and bless humanity?

What makes this doubly hard for God to bear is
that most of His **children** are **"standing all the day
idle,"** and doing very little to **personally** rescue
these perishing people from **hell**.

What more can God do to rescue these from
eternal hell? He has already **paid their sin debt** by
giving His Son to die in their place on the cross.

This is a far worse situation than a farmer losing
his crop. These are people, who are eternal souls! As
such, **they will exist forever** in a horrible place,
which God has prepared for the devil.

64

This is a far worse situation than the terrorist attack that the world witnessed on September 11th. The screams of 9/11 victims were calmed when they were rescued or died. These screams will never be silenced, because in hell they will exist on and on, forever. If they are not reached before they die, they will never stop screaming in the black world of pain and no hope.

IT IS THE ELEVENTH HOUR

It is the **eleventh** hour, the hour of God's **emergency**. After the resurrection of Christ, the hour came for Jesus to leave the apostles alone on the earth. The apostles had to be motivated to give their all, even unto death, in order to get their lost harvest saved.

The screams of 9/11 victims were calmed when they were rescued or died. These screams will never be silenced, because in hell they will exist on and on, forever.

"How can I motivate them so they will lose themselves in the harvest fields?" was the question Jesus faced. His solution was clear. Reveal to them the shortness of the **Kindergarten phase of their lives and show them the eternal glory they will enjoy as they sit on the twelve thrones judging the twelve tribes of Israel during the millennial reign!**[1]

---

[1] See author's book, "Thy Kingdom Come"

65

The apostles were transformed! The world has never since seen the zeal and dedication that the apostles manifested in reaching their generation with the Gospel.

Will it work again? It is the eleventh hour of this dispensation and the harvest day is almost spent.

Most of the eleventh hour believers **are passive**.

Most of them believe that they **cannot** win souls.

Many of them believe **they have disqualified** themselves and God cannot, or will not, use them.

THERE HAS NEVER BEEN SUCH AN EMERGENCY!

"Six billion lost in My vineyard. Six billion precious souls that I gave My Son **TO DIE FOR**," is God's cry.

The need for workers – "This **emergency** can only be helped if there is an **army** of **workers** who will go into My **vineyard**."

Then came the message to the believers who were standing idle, whom the Lord of the harvest was hiring:

"Tell them that I am offering them **three things**."

"**First**, I will give them **amnesty for all of their past failures and mistakes, on the condition that they go to work in My vineyard**."

"**Second, I will pay them the same pay**, or reward, that they would have received if they had worked all their lives for Me, on the condition that they start **winning souls** and getting people saved."

66

"Third, I will never forget them for **answering** My **call** in My **greatest** emergency. At the Judgment Seat, I will promote them to share in My eternal glory, on the condition that **they start getting people saved**."

Sir?

Mom?

Does this make sense to you? It is the 11th hour of this dispensation.

IS THE FOLLOWING TRUE?

- The day is almost over.

- Six billion people need Jesus.

- Most Christians are standing idle.

- God's greatest desire is to save them from hell.

- He has already robbed Heaven of His Son.

- The price has been paid.

"WHY STAND YE HERE ALL THE DAY IDLE?" IS HIS CRY!

THE EMERGENCY IS GREAT!

He will hire you – if you respond to His emergency and GO!

A word of reassurance – Let me reassure you once again. This is only the third lesson in our Kindergarten class. There are still three more startling lessons in this course. If you are one of our serious-minded Kindergarten kids, you will do just fine.

POINTS TO PONDER

- God is working in your life **for your eternal good**.

- The greatest way a Kindergarten kid learns is **through observation**.

- Paul's greatest concern was **to finish his course (purpose) with joy**.

- Solomon's failure was that he lived his life on earth as if it were all there was to life.

- Daniel saw superstars in the millennium who were **those that won souls**.

- **Jesus came to seek and to save sinners**.

- Jesus said, *"As my Father hath sent me, even so send I you."* (John 20:21)

- We are living in the 11th hour, **the hour of Jesus' emergency**.

- Jesus offers amnesty to many, on the condition that they give themselves to the task of winning souls.

LESSON THREE QUESTIONS
The Place To Prepare For Living Is kindergarten

MONDAY – THE PLACE TO PREPARE FOR LIVING IS KINDERGARTEN

1. Most _____ live all their _____ before they _____ what life is all about.

2. As _____ journey through _____, there may be some _____, dark _____ and setbacks.

3. Those _____ were designed for your _____ good.

4. One of the greatest _____ in the Bible is God as your _____ – your daddy.

5. Perhaps the greatest way Kindergarten kids _____ is by _____ of others.

TUESDAY – LEARN FROM A MISSIONARY

1. *"Neither count I my life dear unto _____, so that I might _____ my _____ (purpose) with joy."* (Acts 20:24)

70

2. Find _____ what the _____ was for man's journey through the Kindergarten phase of _____ on this earth.

3. *"The _____ of the righteous is a tree of life; and _____ that _____ souls is _____."* (Proverbs 11:30)

4. God also revealed to _____ those who will be _____ stars under King Jesus.

5. The students in Kindergarten who _____ and are _____ will win _____.

WEDNESDAY – LEARN FROM JESUS

1. When we learn _____ Jesus came to earth and what is _____ to Him, we also _____ what is _____ to Almighty God.

2. *"For the Son of _____ is come to _____ and to _____ that which was lost (sinners)."* (Luke 19:10)

3. In order to _____ to _____, you must experience an inward _____.

4. *"Go _____ to thy friends, and _____ them how great the things of the Lord hath done for_____."* (Mark 5:19)

5. These four _____ are enough to show that Jesus, our _____, came _____ sinners.

THURSDAY – THE CHURCH'S PRIMARY JOB

1. *"Go ye into _____ the world, and _____ the gospel to _____ creature."* (Mark 16:15)

2. *"As my _____ hath sent ____, even so send I _____."* (John 20:21)

3. Six _____ souls are out in the _____ vineyard, and most of them are _____.

4. Most of His _____ are "standing all the day _____", and doing very little to _____ rescue these perishing people from _____.

5. They will never stop _____ in the _____ world of _____ and no _____.

FRIDAY – IT IS THE ELEVENTH HOUR

1. It is the _____ hour, the hour of God's _____.

2. "This _____ can only be helped if there is an _____ of _____ who will go into my _____."

3. "I will give them _____ for all of their past _____ and _____, on the _____ that they go to work in ____ vineyard."

4. "I will never _____ them for _____ my _____ in my _____ emergency."

5. He will _____ you – if you _____ to His _____ and GO!

72

DAILY DECLARATION

Repeat aloud each morning and evening:

"I will strive to be transformed as a Christian by reading and obeying the Word of God each day."

MEMORY VERSE

And be not conformed to this world: but be ye transformed by the renewing of your mind, that ye may prove what is that good, and acceptable, and perfect, will of God. (Romans 12:2)

CHECK BLOCK AFTER REPEATING

	Mon.	Tues.	Wed.	Thurs	Fri.	Sat.	Sun.
A.M.							
P.M.							

I will enlist as a worker in the 11th hour harvest by praying and striving to be a part of a soul-winning effort.

Signature

_____

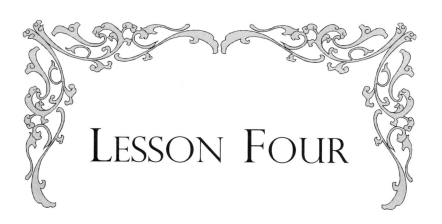

LESSON FOUR

Wherefore the rather, brethren, give diligence and make your calling and election sure: for if ye do these things, ye shall never fail. (2 Peter 1:10)

LESSON FOUR

The Basic Lessons To Be Learned In Kindergarten

In our writing, the Kindergarten phase of life represents the short life span of 70 to 80 years on this earth. Just as **Kindergarten** ends in a gala **graduation**, so does **life** on this earth end with a **graduation** – death. For the good Kindergarten child who has excelled, **it is a time of honor and rewards**. For the person who has accepted this short Kindergarten phase of life and has responded to the teaching and leadership of God, it will also be a time of honor and rewards. Solomon spoke of death as a graduation in Ecclesiastes 7:1, when he wrote,

> *A good name is **better** than precious ointment; and the day of death than the day of one's birth.*

Most people believe that death ends it all. Many speak of a person who just died by saying, "He has gone on to his reward." In this section, we will prove that **both of these statements are false**.

SMART KINDERGARTEN KIDS
REALIZE THAT TIME IS SHORT

The journey through this Kindergarten phase of life compared to eternity is very short. **You will spend far more time on the other side of your physical death than on this side**.

Throughout the Bible, people who lived in previous generations used the following terms to describe the brief span of Kindergarten life:

- The Psalmist, David, said our life is as a **story that is told**. Turn on the television and a story is told in a few minutes and then it is on to the next program.

- James described the briefness of life as the **morning dew**. The sun rises and the dew is gone.

- David **viewed** the duration of life **as a shadow** as it **races** across the countryside and is **gone**.

- The shortness of life is viewed by several writers **as green grass**. With the heat of summer, the grass dies and turns brown.

- A beautiful flower is either **cut down early or withers** a few days later – a dramatic example of life.

- Others have said that life is like a **puff of smoke**. Where did life go?

A smart Kindergarten kid realizes the shortness of Kindergarten and prepares for graduation.

SMART KINDERGARTEN KIDS WORK TO SAVE THEIR LIVES

Jesus admonished the early disciples,

Whosoever will come after me (be my disciple), *let him deny himself (of what he wants to do), and take up his cross* (purpose), *and follow me. For whosoever will save his life* (lives how he wants to live) *shall lose it* (his misspent life); *but whosoever shall lose his life for my sake and the gospel's, the same shall save it* (his life).

*For what shall it **profit** a man, if he shall **gain** the whole world* (becomes **wealthy**), *and lose his own **soul** (**misspends his life**)? Or what shall a man give in exchange for his soul* (his life, to live over again)? (Mark 8:34-37)

Jesus was saying, "If you are going to become a Christian, submit yourself to work out your purpose for which you were saved. But if a person lives his life selfishly and gains tremendous wealth and recognition at the expense of not accomplishing his purpose on earth, what does he have? He will **leave it all behind** when he dies. At the point just before he dies, what would he give to go back and live his life over, and this time fulfill the purpose which God had ordained for his life?"

A smart Kindergarten kid will **learn** to **save** his life by presenting his **body** a living sacrifice to God, and **thus save his life** and fulfill his purpose.

79

SMART KINDERGARTEN KIDS LEARN HOW TO GET THINGS FROM "DADDY"

A little child soon learns how to get things from their Daddy. A smart Kindergarten kid should learn how to get things from his Heavenly Father. We call this process of getting things from our Heavenly Father – prayer.

There are six simple principles that one must follow in order to get their prayers answered:

FIRST: **Pray according to the will of God**. Now, you may ask, "How do I know if I am praying according to God's will?" The answer to your question is, "What are you **praying** for? **Does it glorify God**, or is it just something that you **want**?" There are specific things that God's Word tells us to pray for. If we pray for those things, then we can pray with confidence, knowing our prayers will be answered. Jesus said,

> *And whatsoever ye shall ask in my name, that will I do, that the Father may be glorified in the Son. If ye shall ask any thing in my name, I will do it.* (John 14:13-14)

A smart Kindergarten kid will learn to seek the will of his Father.

SECOND: **Do the things that are pleasing to God**. God tells us to **be kind** to each other. The Bible teaches us to **have compassion** on the poor and unfortunate. Jesus commanded that we are to **seek the salvation** of the lost. Jesus said that we should love people and **take the role** of a servant in helping each other, even in helping strangers.

80

We should **develop** the habit of asking, "**What would Jesus do in this situation?**" and then try to do it.

Why are these things so important for the Kindergarten kid to learn and practice? Listen to the emphatic promise of God to answer your prayers,

> *And whatsoever we ask, we receive of him, because we keep his commandments, and do those things that are pleasing in his sight.* (1 John 3:22)

If we obey His commandments and do the things that we know will please God, we can pray with great confidence.

A smart Kindergarten kid will learn to obey and please his Father.

> And whatsoever we ask, we receive of him, because we keep his commandments, and do those things that are pleasing in his sight. (1 John 3:22)

THIRD: Have faith to keep asking. In Matthew 7:7-8, we have two verses that present what is referred to as the ABC's of prayer:

A – *"Ask, and it shall be given you"*

B – *"Seek, and ye shall find"*

C – *"Knock, and it shall be opened unto you"*

"Ask" means to pray.

"Seek" means to put legs on your prayers and do your part, humanly speaking, to get your prayers answered. An example of this is when we ask God to save a friend who is a sinner. We put legs on our prayers by living a good life before him and talking to him about salvation.

"Knock" means one is to be **persistent** in **asking** and **seeking**, until his **petition** is granted.

A smart Kindergarten kid learns to have faith to keep on knocking (ask, seek) until his prayers are answered.

FOURTH: **Learn to take care of your things**. It is amazing to see the sense of responsibility many children learn at an early age. This is exactly what God, the Father, wants His children to develop – **a sense of responsibility and maturity**. He places small duties into His children's hands to see if He can trust them with more important responsibilities. This is the design He has in training His children to grow and become dependable.

> A smart Kindergarten kid learns to have faith to keep on knocking (ask, seek) until his prayers are answered.

A smart Kindergarten kid will learn to take care of his responsibilities.

FIFTH: **Learn to respect others**. A child learns to respect his personal items and property and to share the things he has. Through learning to respect the rights and property of others, he develops discipline. It is not long before he is helping and teaching his little brother or sister. He soon becomes his brother's protector and role model. This is exactly the level that God is attempting to bring **His** children to – the **level** of **discipline** and **mentoring** younger Christians.

A smart Kindergarten kid will learn to respect and help others.

SIXTH: **Learn the value of money**. A smart Kindergarten kid learns how to save money. A smart Kindergarten kid learns that he can't spend all of his money on candy and ice cream and have anything left to buy more important things. He has to **learn** when to put down **impulses** and say "**No**." This may the hardest lesson a kid has to learn – **how to save and properly spend his money**.

This is also the area in which God has problems with His children. Many of God's children do not want to **listen to what God tells them to do with their money**.

One man said what many must think, "I would do what God said to do with my money, but I never have heard His voice. He has never said anything to me." Evidently, this man **doesn't know how God talks to His children about money** and their investments.

Remember what we have learned:

● God has a good, acceptable and perfect plan **for your life**.

● God works in your life in order for you **to share** in His eternal glory.

Up to this point in your life, God has given you everything. He keeps you alive and gives you the ability to earn. He bought you back from sin's bondage by giving His Son on the cross, and **you are not your own**. We are to glorify Him in our spirit and in our body, which are God's. **Our position is one of stewardship and not one of ownership**.

Now, how did we learn all these truths? We learned these truths by reading the Bible. How does God talk to us about finances, especially about saving and investing our (His) money? He speaks to us the same way, through His written Word.

A smart Kindergarten kid will learn to obey God's Word concerning his money.

Two Very Vivid Commands Concerning Money

In Matthew 6:19-21, Jesus gave two very emphatic commands:

- **The first command is negative.** He said, *"Lay **not** up for yourselves treasures upon earth."* This is in the Bible and He is speaking those words **to all of His Kindergarten kids**.

Then, Jesus gave the logical reasons for us not to invest all of our money in stocks, bonds, houses, land, and other things of this world.

Moth and rust will corrupt, or tarnish, them. They wear out! Things lose their value.

Thieves, including the world's tax system and governing agencies, will take them away or steal them.

84

- **The second command is positive.** *"But lay up for yourselves treasures in heaven."* There **must** be a way for you to lay up your **treasures in Heaven** for Jesus **to have been so emphatic** in His command.

You see, His command is for your good. *"Lay up for yourselves."* This command is in keeping with all of the other principles we have learned. He has designed a good, acceptable and perfect will for your life, which includes saving, or transferring, your earthly treasures into eternal dividends.

How to transfer these funds – Someone said, "Preacher, I would be glad to transfer my treasures into the bank of Heaven if I knew how to do it."

> There must be a way for you to lay up your treasures in Heaven for Jesus to have been so emphatic in His command.

Let us consider another question in answering that statement:

What or who is going to Heaven? Are white-faced cattle, or houses, or barns going to Heaven? **No!** Are stocks and bonds, or the title deeds to land going to Heaven? **No!**

There is only one species on this earth going to Heaven. That is the one that Jesus came down from Heaven and died on the cross to save – man. Men, women, boys and girls are the only eternal beings on this earth. All other things of this world, including this earth, will be burned some day.

The logical conclusion of laying up treasures in Heaven – Since only eternal human beings are the only ones going to Heaven, then in order to lay up treasures in Heaven, **eternal treasures for yourself**, one will have to invest in institutions and people who are working to get people saved from hell to Heaven.

SMART KINDERGARTEN KIDS START A SAVINGS ACCOUNT

Out of the money God enables you to earn, He teaches that you should *"lay by him in store, as God hath prospered"* you. (1 Corinthians 16:2)

He even tells you to start a **weekly savings plan**. Note the first part of 1 Corinthians 16:2. *"Upon the first day of the week (Sunday) let every one of you lay by him in store, as God hath prospered him."* Your Heavenly savings account is called "tithing."

Tithing is taught throughout the Bible. In the Old Testament, long before Mosaic Law was given, God taught that **generation** of Kindergarten kids to **give 10%, or "tithe"**. This is what Abraham gave. Ten percent, or the tithe, is what Jacob (later called Israel) gave. (Genesis 28:20) Israel had twelve sons who became the twelve tribes of Israel. It was over 400 years later that the Law of Moses was given, which required all Jews to tithe.

86

SMART KINDERGARTEN KIDS LEARN FROM THE APOSTLE

The Apostle Paul, in helping people to learn to give of their monies to the Lord, asked the common man a series of simple questions:

● Does a soldier pay his own salary? In 1 Corinthians 9:7, Paul asked some questions that everyone would know the answers to. He asked, *"Who goeth a warfare any time at his own charges?"*

● Does the farmer eat of his grapes? Paul asked, *"Who planteth a vineyard, and eateth not of the fruit thereof?"*

● *Does a herdsman eat of the herd?* The answer is, "Yes," the owner of the herd eats of the flock and drinks of the milk. (verse 7)

● *Does the ox get to eat of the corn?* (verse 9)

The answer from all of the farmers was a resounding, "Yes."

Then Paul applied the logic that he had established. Since everyone who works in the physical realm are partakers of the fruit of their labors, you can understand that those who spend all their time and energy in working in the spiritual work of the Lord should also be paid. In convincing them, he asked them the question,

> *If we have sown unto you spiritual things, is it a great thing if we shall reap your carnal (material) things?* (1 Corinthians 9:11)

87

Then Paul reminded those Jewish members of a truth that they were very familiar with. He said,

> *They which wait* (serve) *at the altar are partakers with the altar.* (verse 13)

The Bible clearly teaches that the altar and temple workers, along with the priests, were supported by the tithes and offerings of the Jewish people.

Even so, or in the same manner described – Then Paul tied all these questions together by stating,

> *Even so hath the Lord ordained that they which preach the gospel should live of the gospel.* (verse 14)

The translated words "even so" are the same words used in John 3:14. *"And as Moses lifted up the serpent in the wilderness, even so must the Son of man be lifted up."* It means "in the same manner," or "in the manner previously described."

Paul's point is referring to the same standard, or way, that the temple workers were supported. *"Even so,...they which preach the gospel should live the gospel."* The standard of support was tithes and offerings.

Later, we will find that God's method of supporting ministries is also **an investment plan**. One supports the preacher, which enables the preacher to devote his full time to the ministry. This enables him to win more souls to the Lord. In the Lord's marvelous computer system, He computes a percentage of the success of the preacher's ministry **into the Heavenly bank account of the investor**. Thus, he shall share in the eternal dividends of the ministries he has supported **in this investor's program**. What a lesson for a little Kindergarten kid to learn!

So, all generations of Kindergarten kids – those before the law of dispensation and those after the law – were taught to start at the same level. God gave them the ability to make 100%. They, in turn, were to lay up for **themselves 10% in Heaven by investing in God's work**.

Thus, he shall share in the eternal dividends of the ministries he has supported in this investor's program.

This is the way God and His Kindergarten kids could become co-laborers together. God **promised** that if His child would invest 10% back into getting people saved, He would bless the 90% and make it go farther than the entire 100% would go if the kid kept it and used it for himself.

The father knows a lot more about money matters than the child, especially when the Father is God. Especially when the Father is working for His child's eternal good!

POINTS TO PONDER

- **You will spend more time** on the other side than on this side of life.

- What profits a man if he gains the whole world but **misspends his life**?

- One can learn to get his prayers answered by being persistent in the knocking.

- The hardest lesson a kid learns is how to save and **properly spend his money**.

- **God keeps you alive and gives you the ability to earn**.

- His command is for your good – *"Lay up for yourselves."*

- God will make the 90% go farther than the 100%.

- Giving is an eternal investment plan and is the way God has ordained for you to **"lay up for yourself treasures in Heaven."**

LESSON FOUR QUESTIONS
The Basic Lessons To Be Learned In Kindergarten

MONDAY – THE BASIC LESSONS TO BE LEARNED

1. Just as _____ ends in a gala _____, so does _____ on this earth end with a _____ – death.

2. *"A good name is* _____ *than precious oint-ment; and the* _____ *of death* (greater) *than the day of one's* _____*."* (Ecclesiastes 7:1)

3. You will _____ far more _____ on the other side of your _____ death than on _____ side.

4. David _____ the duration of life as a _____ as it _____ across the country-side and is _____.

5. Others have said that life is like a _____ of smoke. Where did it go?

Tuesday – Smart Kindergarten Kids Work

1. *"For what shall it _____ a man, if he shall _____ the whole world* (becomes _____), *and lose his own* ____ (_____ his life)?"* (Mark 8:36)

2. A smart Kindergarten kid will _____ to _____ his life by presenting his _____ a living sacrifice to God.

3. "What are you _____ for? Does it _____ God, or is it just something that you _____?"

4. We should _____ the habit of asking, "What _____ Jesus do in _____ situation?"

5. A smart Kindergarten kid will _____ to _____ and _____ his Father.

Wednesday – Have Faith To Keep Asking

1. "Knock" means one is to be _____ in _____ and _____, until his _____ is granted.

2. God is attempting to bring _____ children to the _____ of _____ and _____ younger Christians.

3. He has to _____ when to put down _____ and say "____."

4. Many of God's children do not want to ____ to what God ____ them to ___ with their money.

5. Our _____ is one of _____ and not one of ownership.

THURSDAY – TWO VERY VIVID COMMANDS

1. *"Lay* _____ *up for yourselves treasures upon*
   _____.*"* (Matthew 6:19)

2. There _____ be a way for you to lay up your
   _____ in _____ for Jesus to have been
   so _____ in His command.

3. He has designed a _____, _____ and perfect will for your life, which _____ saving
   your _____ treasures into _____ dividends.

4. _____ other things of this _____, including
   this earth, will be _____ some day.

5. God taught that _____ Kindergarten
   kids to _____ 10%, or "_____.*"*

FRIDAY – APOSTLE PAUL ASKS
KINDERGARTEN QUESTIONS

1. *"Who* _____ *(to) a* _____ *any time at his own*
   _____?*"* (1 Corinthians 9:7)

2. You can _____ that those who spend _____
   their _____ and _____ in working in the
   _____ work of the Lord should also be paid.

3. *"Even* _____ *hath the* _____ *ordained that they*
   which preach the gospel should _____ *of the*
   gospel." (1 Corinthians 9:14)

4. God _____ them the ability to make _____.
   They, in turn, were to _____ up for _____
   10% in Heaven, by _____ in God's work.

5. The _____ knows a lot _____ about money matters than the _____, especially when the _____ is God.

DAILY DECLARATION

Repeat aloud each morning and evening:

"The God who blessed Abraham, Sarah, Caleb, Zacharias and Elisabeth in their old age will bless me if I meet His conditions."

MEMORY VERSE

But the God of all grace, who hath called us unto his eternal glory by Christ Jesus, after that ye have suffered a while, make you perfect, stablish, strengthen, settle you. (1 Peter 5:10)

CHECK BLOCK AFTER REPEATING

	Mon.	Tues.	Wed.	Thurs	Fri.	Sat.	Sun.
A.M.							
P.M.							

I will strive to do the things that I have learned so I can fulfill God's will of laying up treasures in Heaven.

Signature

_____

LESSON
FIVE

*But grow in grace, and in the knowl-
edge of our Lord and Saviour Jesus
Christ. To him be glory both now and
for ever. Amen.* (2 Peter 3:18)

LESSON FIVE

An Advanced Lesson To Be Learned For Leadership

All parents like for their **kids** to do **well** and **excel**. There is nothing that makes mom and dad any prouder than **a good report card**, or when their child is singing and **starring** in the school play. That will bring the whole clan out – both sets of grandparents, uncles and aunts, even shirt-tail cousins will be there to watch their little star perform. And if there is a **little star, or leader**, in the Kindergarten class, someone at home is encouraging him on.

Where did we human **beings** get this **nature**? Why is it that parents are the happiest when their child is doing well? Maybe it is not in academics that their child excels. It may be in Little League, or kicking that little round ball on the soccer field. Regardless of where the parents are receiving fulfillment from their child, **there is a natural tendency** for them to be there, rooting him on to higher achievement.

Again, the basic nature of our being to root on our children **comes from our Heavenly Father**, because we were made in His image and likeness. There has never been a father who aspires greatness for his kids more than our Heavenly Father.

One of the most God-like characteristics is **giving**.

For God so loved the world, that he gave...."
(John 3:16)

> There has never been a father who aspires greatness for his kids more than our Heavenly Father.

The love God has compels Him to give. There is not one good thing on this earth but that God gave it. It has been said that one can give without loving, but it is impossible for one to love without giving. So, if one is to develop and become a leader among God's Kindergarten kids, he must grow in the grace of giving.

THE LAST ADMONITION OF THE FIRST PASTOR

The Apostle Peter became the first pastor after Jesus was promoted back to Heaven. He was personally trained by Jesus and was the most successful leader and pastor, perhaps that the world has ever seen. When he was an old man and ready to die, Jesus asked him to send a message to all of His Kindergarten kids. Peter concluded his last message by saying,

*But **grow** in **grace**, and in the **knowledge** of our Lord and Saviour Jesus Christ.* (2 Peter 3:18)

FAITH GIVING

The **command** of growing in grace (enabling ability) and knowledge (of God's purpose for our life) has **led** many of God's children to enter into the practice of "**FAITH GIVING**". Faith giving is practiced by the advanced members of this Kindergarten class. They have learned and practiced giving the first 10%, and oftentimes a far larger percentage, back to God each week. In addition, they give offerings as well. Those who give regularly of their tithes and offerings have ventured into the exciting way of **FAITH GIVING**.

Faith giving is practiced by the advanced members of this Kindergarten class.

The church that practices faith giving sets aside a period of time where people fast and pray about God's will in their lives as faithful stewards over God's heritage.

Their particular prayer is for God to reveal to them an additional amount (grow in grace and knowledge) to give "**BY FAITH**" over and above what they are already giving. Their prayer is:

"God, lay on my heart that amount that You will supply to me each week over and above what I am already giving. And as You supply the additional money I will, by faith, give it.

99

This is a way I can grow in grace, and at the **same time, lay up treasures in Heaven.**"

Grow in grace (enabling ability) and knowledge (of God and His work). As we grow and learn more about life, especially the principle that **this life is the Kindergarten phase of our eternal journey**, we learn to invest far more than the simple 10%.

Paul said, "Sow a little, reap a little, and have a little in the bank of Heaven. Sow a lot, reap a lot, as you lay up a lot in the bank of Heaven." And at the rate of 100-fold return (10,000% growth) on your investment, as promised, on some investments you will reap a high eternal return.

A GREAT BANK ACCOUNT

✝

Sow a little, reap a little, and have a little in the bank of Heaven.

Those who are smart in this Kindergarten phase of life should learn how to obey Jesus' admonition of laying up treasures in Heaven. When one **obeys** that command, **he will not leave it all behind** when he graduates, but will have a great Heavenly bank account and a good start on his journey **through the millennial Kingdom**.

Not only does the smart Kindergarten kid learn how to give more liberally as he becomes more like Jesus, but he **learns how to enjoy his money**. Money, in itself, is neither **good nor evil**. Money, in itself, can bring much pain, or it can produce unending joy. A **smart** Kindergarten kid **studies** to learn how to use money so he will **enjoy** it.

MONEY, IN ITSELF, CAN BRING MUCH PAIN

Solomon is the man to whom God gave unlimited wealth, which made him the richest man in the world during his lifetime. Solomon's job was to **find** out how to **use** riches **in order to be happy**. During his experiment, he discovered that money, in itself, can bring to its owner **much pain**.

The apostle Paul said the love of money is what caused many Christians to err from the faith. The end result of coveting riches is described by Paul as:

One piercing himself through with many sorrows (pain). (1 Timothy 6:10)

Please observe some truths about money:

1. **Attainment of riches does not satisfy.** Solomon said that those who made a lot of money weren't satisfied with what they had. They wanted to make more. When they achieved more, it created a hunger for more. That hunger was replaced with a greater desire to take the business to a "higher level." Solomon said,

   He that loveth silver shall not be satisfied with silver; nor he that loveth abundance with increase: this is also vanity. (Ecclesiastes 5:10)

   Solomon also observed that the more one makes, the greater costs there are in obtaining

101

and maintaining it. The only satisfaction one has in his wealth is in the fact that he can see it and say, **"That belongs to me."**

*"When goods increase, they are increased that eat them: and what good is there to the owners thereof, **saving the beholding of them with their eyes?"** (That's mine!) (Ecclesiastes 5:11)

Those riches also cost the owners a lot of sleepless nights.

But the abundance of the rich man will not suffer him to sleep. (verse 12)

2. **Money can become a curse.** Solomon also stated that money that was horded up and not properly used could become very hurtful.

*There is a sore evil which I have seen under the sun, namely, **riches kept for the owners thereof to their hurt.*** (Ecclesiastes 5:13)

A WARNING TO THE WEALTHY

In James 4:17, the Bible clearly states that,

*Him that knoweth to do good, and doeth it not, to **him it is sin**.*

Then comes one of the most scathing warnings found in the Bible **to people who have misspent their wealth**.

James 5:1 begins,

*Go to now, ye rich men, weep and howl for your miseries that **shall come upon you**.*

Judgment will come as they stand defenseless before their God. They had been all powerful in their own little worlds. They acted like the owner, the creator; and did what would further their own interests. They ignored the plain statement of the Bible,

> *The earth is the Lord's, and the fullness thereof.* (Psalm 24:1)

They ignored the fact that He created all things; that through His power all things "consist" and are held together. They acted like the owner of all things, instead of the steward over the things that God gave them to manage. The statement "weep and howl" 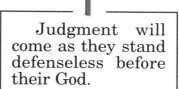 shows the severity of their judgment as He takes from them their misused talents, and places them (those who have been saved) into servitude during the millennium – where they will reap what they have sown in the lives of those whom they mistreated.

Judgment will come as they stand defenseless before their God.

James 5:2 continues,

> *Your riches are corrupted, and your garments are moth-eaten.*

The things that the rich treasure the most are useless and ruined.

The admonition continues in James 5:3:

> *Your gold and silver (that God had given them to use) is cankered; and the rust of them shall*

be a witness against you, and shall eat your flesh as it were fire.

The very things they treasured the most will turn on them and be their condemnation. Please note the final sentence in this verse: *"Ye have heaped treasure together for the last days."* This is referring to the last days of their lives, when they wanted to live in luxurious retirement.

James 5:4 gives the reason for the angry judgment of God toward those who misused their wealth:

Behold, the hire of the labourers who have reaped down your fields, which is of you kept back by fraud, crieth: and the cries of them which have reaped are entered into the ears of the Lord of sabaoth.

The wealthy ones, whom God was very angry with, are the ones who did not pay their employees properly. They made them work overtime without pay. They failed to pay bonuses when their workers made them high profits. They kept them on starvation wages. God watched over all of their selfishness and saw the meager existence of the workers. He saw the tears and heartache of those poor, struggling families, while the wealthy wasted more money than their employees made.

In James 5:5, God charged them with living in pleasure on earth as victorious conquerors who have destroyed their opponents. The conquering soldiers do just about anything they choose to do to the poor victims, with little concern for their feelings or welfare.

In James 5:6, He charged them with killing and condemning the just, who were unable, or had chosen not to resist them. One may ask, "How did the rich condemn and kill people?" God gave people wealth in order to get the Gospel out to a lost world. When they hoarded and misused the wealth that God had enabled them to accumulate, instead of supporting the missionaries, the masses that would have been reached through the Gospel remained condemned. They died because the provision to reach them was selfishly perverted from being used to save their eternal lives. Now, they were dead (separated from God), in hell, and God charged those who could have reached them, but didn't, with murder.

In James 5:7, God encouraged His children and the poor of the earth, who have been abused and mistreated, to be patient because the husbandman (real owner of the earth) is coming to intervene and judge their abusers.

A SON WHO LABORED FOR THE WIND

In Ecclesiastes, chapter 5, Solomon identified a very hurtful example of how money that has been hoarded up and not properly used could become very hurtful. He used the example of a child born of wealthy parents who had programmed him from infancy to take over the family business. The son is obedient and spends all his life running and directing the business. He lives his whole life, works his whole life, for the company position he inherited. Solomon's summation was that the son *"laboured for the wind,"* because he came into the world naked and left the world **naked**. The indication is that the son, because of being programmed to run the family business, **died in darkness** (was not saved). The money that the parents left to the son became a curse instead of a blessing. (Ecclesiastes 5:14-17) The good intentions of the parents for the security and well-being of their child became a curse, instead of a blessing.

THE GREATEST BLESSING TO ME

The following, no doubt, will be one of the most unusual examples you have ever read. The year before your author was born, his father was on the verge of becoming a very wealthy man. He worked as a contractor in the Texas oil fields. He was clearing large sums of money every day. His company was well-known and well-respected. The future was very bright indeed, and then the greatest **blessing to the author** (before I was even born) **happened**.

> The money that the parents left to the son became a curse instead of a blessing. (Ecclesiastes 5:14-17)

My dad, who seldom labored with his men, worked on a Saturday morning when one of his men failed to show up for work. There was a terrible accident, which broke 28 bones in my dad's body, including his back. They thought, at first, that he would die before arriving at the hospital. God intervened and, after 242 days in the hospital, he was released. His company was bankrupt; his money was all gone. He had only enough money to buy a 320-acre farm in Oklahoma near a veterans' hospital.

I was born while my father was still in the hospital in Texas. We moved to Oklahoma when I was six months old. My father could not walk, much less work. But my four older brothers had been trained to work. Over the next nine years, they worked along with my father, who was slowly regaining his health, to build this 320-acre farm into another successful business. Then, a second tragedy struck. A fire bird (arsonist) burned down three huge, picturesque barns in a week's time. Ours was the second. Along with the barn went all the year's crops. The insurance had recently expired and all was lost. My mother's health (asthma) had gotten so bad that the doctors ordered her to a better climate. We left Oklahoma with barely the clothes on our backs.

You are wondering, "How could those two major tragedies be counted **the greatest blessing in my life**?"

Some may say, "What a sick sense of humor."

Another may state, "What a perverted view of life."

An Explanation Is In Order

My nature is one of intense loyalty to my friends and, especially, my family. There are genes, which I received at birth from my parents and grandparents, to excel in life. Within me is a driving force to please my parents and excel above my contemporaries.

If my father had continued to excel in life and had trained his sons in his lucrative business (which he would have), if I had earned a position of leadership in his company, then my nature would have compelled me to develop the company into one of the nation's greatest. I would have been consumed in building the business. Everything else, including God's purpose for my life, would have received no consideration from me.

The sum total of my life would have been described as "one who labored for the wind," and I would have gone out of this life in darkness, lost and condemned to hell forever.

Now can you understand why I consider these two major tragedies to be the greatest blessing of my life?

MONEY CAN GIVE FALSE HOPE

> The sum total of my life would have been described as "one who labored for the wind."

When parents leave their riches to their children, they think they are setting up their children to really live and be somebody. But in reality, the children receive very little lasting good from it. Some go on one continuous party until the inheritance is gone. Others assume an air of smugness, as if they are better than other people. Those who want to follow in their parents' footsteps become slaves to their inheritance (the family business) and misspend the rest of their lives in pursuit of a life that cannot bring happiness and satisfaction. They discover that they don't have a business, the business has them. This all starts when the parents fail to recognize the Kindergarten phase of life in comparison to eternity. Secondly, the parents fail to recognize that it was God who gave them the ability, desire and perseverance to work hard, sacrifice and build their wealth. They take all or most of the credit for their accomplishments and mistakenly assume the role of ownership instead of stewardship. The story in Luke 12:16-21 is a perfect example of someone who allowed his driving desire to wreck his life. He built barns, then added greater barns, and upon completing his accomplishments said to himself, "Now, retire and take life easy because you are fixed financially and have security for the rest of your life."

> "Now, retire and take life easy because you are fixed financially and have security for the rest of your life."

God said to him the same night,

Thou fool, this night thy soul shall be required of thee: then whose shall those things be, which thou hast provided? (Luke 16:20)

God gave this warning because all men have the tendency to covet and build things for themselves. With this mistaken conviction, they compound their problem by leaving their worldly riches to their children.

PROPER USE OF MONEY
CAN BRING MUCH HAPPINESS

Again, in considering life, may we remind the reader that God's overall purpose for His Kindergarten children is for them to have a good, acceptable and perfect purpose. Jesus came that one could have life and have it more abundantly, and God's overall will is to develop you so you can share in His eternal glory.

Who gives one wealth? Again, Solomon said that it is God who gave man *"riches, wealth, and honor."* (Ecclesiastes 6:2) A man once said, "I earned my money the hard way. God didn't give me a thing."

Please answer this question. "Who gave you your life, your brain, your energy, your business plan, etc.?"

It was God.

The **beautiful** part about giving it to you is that **He wanted you to enjoy** your riches, **wealth** and honor. There is a way for you to obtain that enjoyment from your money.

In the book of Ecclesiastes, where most of Solomon's experiments end up described as **"vanity and vexation of spirit,"** there is one that begins by the statement, **"Attention!"** It has the same connotation as when an army officer walks into a room of enlisted men. Someone shouts, **"Attention!"** Upon this command, every enlisted man stands and gives his full attention. This is the case when Solomon began a statement concerning riches and wealth.

He said, "Behold (**Attention!**) *that which I have seen: it is good and comely* (pleasant).*"* (Ecclesiastes 5:18)

What is it that Solomon wanted us to focus all of our attention on that was so good?

110

It was,

> *For one to eat and to drink, and to enjoy the good of all his labour that he taketh under the sun all the days of his life, which God giveth him: **for it is his portion.*** (Ecclesiastes 5:18)

Solomon was saying that the portion he receives is to learn to enjoy his riches by following God's leadership in doing good with his money.

In simple terms, God has a **way** for man to really **enjoy** the financial **increase** of his labor.

In the next verse, Solomon stated that,

> *God hath given riches and wealth, and hath given him power to eat thereof, and to take his portion, and to rejoice in his labour.*

Then he made the statement,

> *This is the gift of God.* (Ecclesiastes 5:19)

What Solomon was saying is that God gives men power (ability and authority) to obtain riches and wealth to use for the purpose of laying up treasures for themselves in Heaven. They do this by investing in God's works and helping those who are less fortunate.

They become a channel of blessing to their fellow man. **God gives them** riches and wealth **so they can use it in blessing and helping in the Lord's work**.

The wording of verse twenty makes the verse difficult to understand.

Solomon said,

For he (the one with wealth) shall not much remember the days of his life; because God answereth him in the joy of his heart.

He was saying that a wealthy person will not remember one day over another day **as being the happiest** or most enjoyable day of his life. This is because every day God so blesses him in his heart and life that he cannot single out **any one time over another time**, because all of them **have been so blessed and rewarding**. This verse teaches that people with wealth can also live an abundant life and be among the happiest people alive.

> God so blesses him in his heart and life that he cannot single out any one time over another time, because all of them have been so blessed and rewarding.

God gives him wealth, which he gives back to God as he uses it for God's work. God blesses him in his heart and gives him another increase, which he promptly gives to further another one of God's projects. On and on he goes, and he not only receives riches and wealth, **but honor**. Those that are blessed by his gift **render him proper recognition and honor**. A person who has wealth receives a double blessing when he teaches his son how to enjoy his wealth by using it to bless and help win lost humanity.

All of that is good, but when you consider that God's interest rate is sometimes 30 or 60 times the investment, or even 100-fold – which means the interest rate becomes 10,000 times the amount invested – **it staggers the mind**. No wonder Jesus said, _"Lay not up for yourselves treasures upon earth,"_ because you will get **little or no return** from it. Other times, laying up treasures on this earth will be to your hurt. But lay up for yourselves treasures in Heaven's bank by giving to the Lord's work, where you will get an unbelievable return on your money and it will be an **everlasting** inheritance.

Every smart Kindergarten kid who advances above his classmates learns how to be more mature in saving and investing his money. He learns to **look** beyond the **short Kindergarten phase of his life** and invest in things that will transpire after he graduates. When he does this, it is evident that he has advanced to the head of his class and will have a good report card to show his Heavenly Father when he gets home.

The author promised in a previous lesson that each person was capable of winning souls – that you, personally, could be a part in winning souls to Christ. In our final lesson, we will present some startling information that shows your great potential in influencing many people to be saved.

Points To Ponder

● Our Heavenly Father **wants you to do well** and have a good report card.

● But in order to do well, **you must continue** to grow in grace (enabling ability) and knowledge.

● A proper understanding that this life is the Kindergarten phase of our earthly journey helps one to invest wisely.

● God wants you to enjoy **the financial increase** of your labor.

● The **good intentions** of the parents for the security and well-being of their son **became a curse**.

● Parents failed **to recognize that it was God who gave** the ability, desire and perseverance to accumulate wealth.

● A father has great satisfaction when he teaches his son **how to enjoy and invest money**.

LESSON FIVE QUESTIONS
An Advanced Lesson To Be Learned For Leadership

MONDAY – AN ADVANCED LESSON TO BE LEARNED

1. All parents like for their _____ to do _____ and _____.

2. Where did we human _____ get that _____?

3. There is not one good _____ on this _____ but that God _____ it.

4. If one is to develop and become a _____ among God's Kindergarten kids, he must _____ in the _____ of giving.

5. *"But _____ in _____, and in the _____ of our Lord and Saviour Jesus Christ."* (2 Peter 3:18)

TUESDAY – FAITH GIVING

1. The _____ of growing in grace has _____ many of God's children to enter into the practice of "_____ giving."

115

2. They have _____ and giving the first ____%, and often times a far larger _____, back to God _____ week.

3. This is a _____ I can _____ in grace, and at the same time, _____ up treasures in _____.

4. Paul said, "Sow a _____, reap a _____, and _____ a _____ in the bank of Heaven."

5. _____ a lot, _____ a lot.

WEDNESDAY – A GREAT BANK ACCOUNT

1. When one _____ that command, ____ will _____ leave it _____ behind when he graduates.

2. A _____ Kindergarten kid _____ to learn how to use money so he will _____ it.

3. Solomon's job was to _____ out how to _____ riches in order to be _____.

4. The ____ result of coveting riches is _____ by Paul as: *"one _____ himself through with many _____ (pain) ."*(1 Timothy 6:10)

5. The _____ satisfaction one has is his _____ is in the fact that he can see it and say, "_____ belongs to ____."

THURSDAY – MONEY CAN BECOME A CURSE

1. *"There is a _____ evil which I have _____ under the sun, namely, _____ kept for the owners thereof to their _____."* (Ecclesiastes 5:13)

2. Solomon's summation was that the son "_____ for the _____," because he came into the world _____ and left the world _____.

3. When the _____ leave their _____ to their children, they think they are setting up their children to really _____ and ____ somebody.

4. Others _____ an air of smugness, as if they are _____ than other people.

5. Proper _____ of _____ can _____ much happiness.

FRIDAY – WHO GIVES ONE WEALTH?

1. The _____ part about giving it to you is that He _____ you to _____ your riches, _____ and honor.

2. God has a _____ for man to really _____ the financial _____ of his labor.

3. God _____ them riches and wealth so they can ____ it in _____ and help in the _____ work.

4. By _____ to the Lord's _____, where you will get an _____ return on your money and it will be an _____ inheritance.

5. He learns to _____ beyond the _____ Kindergarten phase of his _____ and invest in things that will _____ after he graduates.

DAILY DECLARATION

Repeat aloud each morning and evening:

"I will strive to avail myself to the God of all grace so He can work out is His perfect plan in my life."

MEMORY VERSE

For we are his workmanship, created in Christ Jesus unto good works, which God hath before ordained that we should walk in them. (Ephesians 2:10)

CHECK BLOCK AFTER REPEATING

	Mon.	Tues.	Wed.	Thurs	Fri.	Sat.	Sun.
A.M.							
P.M.							

I will accept God's plan for enjoying my money by giving as He leads me to give.

Signature

_____

LESSON SIX

And I heard a voice from heaven saying unto me, Write, Blessed are the dead which die in the Lord from henceforth: Yea, saith the Spirit, that they may rest from their labours; **and their works do follow them**. (Revelations 14:13)

LESSON SIX

The Way To Keep Working After Kindergarten

We have finally arrived in our Kindergarten class, and are ready to learn how to keep working (laying up treasures in Heaven) after we graduate.

We graduate from our Kindergarten phase of life by dying. The **Bible** teaches that although you **die** physically, **you can keep working**, even though your **body** is in the **grave**. If we are going to continue to work after death, then we are going to have to make good choices before graduation.

In order to keep working after we die, we are going to have to make investments **in people and projects** that will keep working on this earth, even though we have left this earth by graduation.

> If we are going to continue to work after death, then we are going to have to make good choices before graduation.

THE BEST INVESTMENTS ARE IN PEOPLE

People are alive! They were created in the likeness of God and are visionary and creative. When one invests his riches in people who have the possibility of winning thousands, or possibly even millions, of souls to Christ – what an investment!

The Philippian church invested in Paul's ministry. In Philippians 4:15, Paul spoke of the Philippian church sending him offering after offering. Paul was thrilled to have their investments into his ministry and church planting work. He said,

> *Not because I desire a gift* (your money): *but I desire fruit* (your investment, which won souls) *that may abound to your account* (bank of Heaven). (Philippians 4:17)

The church sponsored Paul's mission works by supporting him financially. Paul won many **souls** to Christ and the **church** was **rewarded** by God with **partial** credit for their salvation. This partial payment was then deposited into their Heavenly bank account.

Please note one word, "abound". Take one grain of corn and plant it. In the corn belt, many stalks produce one or two ears of corn that have 300 kernels on them. Shell that corn and use it for seed corn the following year.

Note that one grain of corn becomes 300 stalks of corn, and each produces one or two ears of corn, which produce 300 kernels each. Repeat the process again and again and you have the definition of the word "abound."

What an investment! Can you imagine the return the Philippian church received from their support of Paul's ministry? No wonder Jesus speaks of the return into **some ministry** as 30 fold, 60 fold, and sometimes as high as 100 fold. (Matthew, chapter 13) From one grain of corn comes tens of thousands of ears of corn!

Two Old Widows Invested In A Young Preacher

A young Bible college student was invited to have tea with two old widows whose husbands had been pastors. After some cookies and tea, the widows inquired about the young man's future plans.

The young man had no money or any promise of any money, but he had a strong conviction that God wanted him to pursue the calling into the ministry by attending Seminary for further training. Without hesitation, he answered, "I am going to the Seminary."

"Our husbands would want us to invest this in your ministry (one grain of corn)."

"Good," came one widow's reaction. "We were hoping you would say that."

When the young preacher boy left, each of the widows gave him an envelope. "Our husbands would want us to invest this in your ministry (one grain of corn)."

To his shock, **J. Vernon McGee** found two checks of $500 each in the envelopes. **Dr. J. Vernon McGee**

123

became a successful pastor, author, television and radio speaker. Millions upon millions have heard his voice on the radio during their lifetime as he continued teaching *"Through the Bible."*

✝

Every time a soul is saved by hearing a J. Vernon McGee message, a portion of the credit goes to their accounts.

Today, the two widows are in Heaven along with that preacher boy in whom they invested. Dr. J. Vernon McGee's books are still being used by multitudes and, although he is **dead** (graduated), he is **still** heard on over 1000 **radio** stations **worldwide** every day.

Those two widows who took part of their deceased husbands' money are resting in Heaven. Their investment is still working today. Every time a soul is saved by hearing a J. Vernon McGee message, a portion of the credit goes to their accounts. Now that is a perfect example of how one grain of corn can be compounded and be described as "fruit that can abound to your heavenly account."

HOW TO INVEST YOUR MONEY

There may be someone who is thinking, "That is all well and good for someone who has money, but how about a person on a fixed income like me?"

Before answering that question, let me ask you a question or two.

"Was your life up until this point easy? Was everything handed to you on a **silver platter**? No, I didn't

124

think so. You had to work for everything you have. You had to earn it. Sometimes you worked **while in pain**, or when you were **sick**. Remember those days when you thought **you couldn't make it to quitting time**? Then you had to go home and take care of your family obligations. You worked because you knew the consequences of giving into your feelings and the problems that would create.

Many have lost their purpose to work and now give in to their aches and pains. The **result** of giving in to their aches and pains is that they have lost their **purpose** to live and are **just waiting to die**. Does this sound like the plan that was described as **a good, acceptable, and perfect plan for your life**?

Because you didn't make much money, you didn't have much to give back to the Lord and lay up treasures in your Heavenly savings account? Now you can see that you could have given more if you had understood these principles better.

You are still alive, aren't you? You can still work a few hours a week, can't you? You respond by saying, "I don't know if I can or not."

Let me put it another way. You could still work a few hours a week **if God gave you the strength** and grace to do it, couldn't you?

You will never know if you can or not until you ask Him to help you, and then try it. Now, you would be **working** to "**lay up treasures**" for yourself by investing in the **Lord's** work.

Do you know that you are commanded to do so? Your response is, "Where in the Bible does it teach that I should work so I can support and invest in the Lord's cause?"

In Acts 20:34-35, Paul said,

> *Yea, ye yourselves know, that these hands have ministered unto my (his own) necessities, and to them that were with me.* (Paul worked to help support the missionaries with him.) *I have showed you all things, how that so labouring ye ought to support the weak, and to remember the words of the Lord Jesus, how he said, "It is more blessed to give than to receive."*

There it is. *"You ought to support the weak."* They are young men who are weak in the faith. They are struggling to make it to Bible college. They are worn out physically; they are stressed out mentally; and they are about to "throw in the towel." They can't pay their tuition and are behind on other bills. The Bible commands that there are some Christians who should help them. You adopt a young man, like J. Vernon McGee, and you will rejoice forever as he perseveres and wins thousands to Christ. You will learn what Jesus meant when He said, *"It is more blessed to give than to receive."* Friend, you are going to die! Get out of your self-centered thinking and get up and do something while you are still alive.

> Do you think Jesus ever suffered while **working for you**?

Do you think Jesus ever suffered while **working for you**? How about when He was in the garden of Gethsemane (He sweat great drops of blood), or on the cross of Calvary? Did He hurt while doing His work **to save lost souls**? Do you think it would be acceptable for **your old muscles to ache** a little bit in order to make money to invest in a young preacher who, like J. Vernon McGee, will be preaching long after your graduation?

MY MOTHER'S EXAMPLE

My old mother, in her seventies and on a fixed income, would fast or **miss a meal or two** in order to lay up for herself treasures in Heaven by giving to missions. She probably never thought about laying up treasures for herself in Heaven when she gave. She just computed what some meals a week would cost, and gave that money to the Lord **to be used in missions**.

Please do not misunderstand me. God looks at what one has and the sacrifice it may be for someone to give a small offering. Once when my wife and I needed quite a bit of money to go on a mission trip, we asked people to prayerfully consider investing in our soul-winning effort. We appreciated the smallest offering the most. It was from a crippled lady who almost didn't help because her gift was so small. She gave it anyway. We appreciated it and were blessed because we knew how much it had cost her. Of all the monies we received, it may have been the only true sacrifice that anyone made in order to help us.

Hey, your old body is going to hurt a little bit when you get old. You can give in to your aches and pains and let the world go to hell without ever suffering any pain by trying to save people; or you can become a smart Kindergartener and work so you can invest in people who will keep working after your graduation. As you get older, your old body is going to ache. You can suffer discomfort while working on a job in order to have money to invest in your eternal bank account, or you can give in to your aches and pains and do nothing. Either way, your body is going to ache. One way, you have a purpose for getting out of bed. The other way, you lament about your aches and pains until you die. When you are unable to physically labor any more, you still have a job to do. It is a very important job. Your life's work is not over on this earth.

You respond to this by asking, "What can a tired, worn out, old person like me do?"

FIRST: Get off the pity party.

SECOND: Realize that God still has work for you to do, because you are still alive.

THIRD: There are people who need your example as a Christian. As you suffer, you can manifest the love and tenderness of Christ. Become a good role model of what a Christian is and how a Christian acts in adverse conditions.

FOURTH: There are people, including your family, who you can tell about your wonderful Savior. Have you ever suffered any in order to get some sinner saved from hell? Here is your chance.

FIFTH: You can pray. In fact, the Bible commands, "Pray without ceasing."

PARENTS, PAY ATTENTION

This principle is the principle upon which God intended the home to be established. Parents are to train Godly children who will multiply **their parents' investment** by winning souls and living dedicated lives long after their parents graduate from this life.

A GREAT INVESTMENT IS IN INSTITUTIONS

One cannot improve on what the Bible teaches. When one finds a **biblical** principle concerning any **facet** of life and **follows** it, then he is **assured** of success.

The principle of investing one's wealth in an institution is a Biblical principle. It was practiced by the first church in the book of Acts.

The command of Jesus to His church – In Matthew 28:18-20, Jesus commanded the apostles to teach or train their disciples well enough so that their converts would be able to teach and train others.

3000 new members in one day – On the Day of Pentecost, there were multitudes of people, from seventeen different countries, in Jerusalem for that great Jewish holiday. Three thousand of those out-of-town guests got saved and baptized. (Acts 2:41-42)

If the apostles were going to teach those converts so well that they could teach others, then it meant the 3000 were going to **have to stay in Jerusalem for a period of time**. That meant food, tons of food. The question arose, "Where will we get enough food to feed these people, along with hundreds more who are getting saved every week?"

Acts 2:44-45 gives the answer for temporary relief:

And all that believed were together, and had **all things common;** *and sold their possessions and goods, and parted them to all men,* **as every man had need**.

Read the next three verses and you will see the joy, happiness, praise and fellowship that they had. It was a marvelous time: friends, neighbors and family members all getting saved, then baptized, and then on to classes in the Bible college at the church. They all experienced the excitement of **on-the-job training from house to house**, as the apostles perfected their new converts to win and disciple people.

But it became apparent that the training institution was going to have to shut down unless God worked some kind of miracle. They had run out of food.

A huge investment in Heaven's bank – As the sacrificial sharing of homes, food and clothing was running low, God moved on one man's heart to transfer his physical assets into spiritual, eternal dividends.

A man who had riches and wealth – In an earlier section of this writing, we showed that the Bible states how God gave riches, wealth and honor. (Ecclesiastes 6:2) This man, whom God had enabled to obtain riches and wealth, sold his land and brought the money to the apostles. The description of *"laid it* *at the apostle's feet"* indicates that it was a lot of money. (Acts 4:36-37)

The institution not only continued its operation, but thousands of others were fed and trained, and the ministry was greatly expanded. Soon after, God added honor to this wealthy man's obedience of laying up treasures in Heaven by investing in the church's

> The description of *"laid it at the apostle's feet"* indicates that it was a lot of money.

training program. Soon, thousands of trained workers were going everywhere, preaching the Word and establishing new churches.

God added the honor – When this little known man, named Joses, gave this huge investment to the Lord, his name was soon changed to Barnabas. Barnabas became one of the most honored and respected Christians in the whole Bible. He is referred to by the Holy Spirit as a good man – full of the Spirit, full of faith. The people of the city of Antioch, who beheld his Godly life, began to refer to him and his followers as "Christians," or Christ-like. He was used by God to later disciple Saul, who became the great apostle Paul. He also discipled Mark, who wrote the Gospel of Mark. He was first given riches and wealth, which he gave back to God. In return, God raised him up to a place of honor that few people will ever attain.

It all started when he was obedient to see the eternal need that could be filled if he was willing to transfer his earthly assets into spiritual, eternal investments. This act of obedience and faith caused Barnabas to become one of the greatest and most honored Christians of all time.

What a lesson for a Kindergarten kid to learn.

Let us consider another Scripture that will enforce this truth of how to keep working after we graduate from this Kindergarten phase of life.

A GREAT INVESTMENT

And I (John) *heard a voice from heaven saying unto me, Write, Blessed are the dead which die in the Lord from henceforth: Yea, saith the Spirit, that they may rest from the labours; and their works do follow them.* (Revelations 14:13)

See that word, *"Blessed"*? It means happy, or good news, or you are in a special place, or a special person. A person who people look up to, desiring to be in your place, or to receive your blessing.

What is this blessed announcement that would cause people to want to be that person?

A person dies in the Lord, meaning they are saved and go to Heaven. There, in Heaven, they are resting in peace and fellowship. They are having a good time, while enjoying a splendid vacation.

Now, the Holy Spirit gets so excited about the good news that He bursts right in and makes the announcement Himself.

What is the announcement that the Holy Spirit cannot contain and has to make Himself? This unbelievable announcement is about God's greatest savings plan!

You, the saints, have graduated to Heaven and are enjoying the greatest vacation that anyone has ever taken. And...

While you are resting in Heaven, your works are still working on earth. Your works are still compounding on earth. Your works are still multiplying on earth.

You sold some property and built a church, and hundreds are being saved. **It goes into your Heavenly account.**

Or you established a scholarship fund to train young preachers and they are winning thousands. **And it goes into your account.**

> While you are resting in Heaven, your works are still working on earth.

Or you enabled a church to build a youth camp, and through that ministry lives are changed and thousands are being saved. **And it goes into your account.**

You are up there basking in the Savior's love and your works are compounding on earth; and all of those dividends will be concluded at the Judgment Seat of Christ, where you will be commended.

Jesus will say,

Well done, thou good and faithful servant: thou hast been faithful over a few things, I will make thee ruler over many things: enter thou into the joy of thy lord. (Matthew 25:21)

A GIFT THAT HAS BEEN COMPOUNDING FOR 100 YEARS

A 100 Year-Old Savings Account

> God gave it to us and we have tried to use it for His glory. We know He will get greater glory if we give it back to Him.

Back a hundred years ago, a young pastor could not get his deacons and leaders to build a building that would accommodate the people they were winning. When it looked like the church would vote down the pastor's request, **an old man and his wife obeyed the Lord**.

God impressed upon their hearts to sell their beautiful little home and give the money to the building fund. When Martha stood and spoke for her husband, Will, she said, "Will and I are going to sell our little house and give the money to the Lord. God gave it to us and we have tried to use it for His glory. We know He will get greater glory if we give it back to Him."

The church became deadly quiet. Silence hung over the crowd as they pondered her announcement, until it was broken by the sobs of those present. Person after person stood, and soon all of the money was raised.

134

Will and Martha soon sold their treasured home and invested the money into the **FIRST BAPTIST CHURCH of DALLAS, TEXAS**. Thus, a little country church was transformed into one of the most mighty churches in America and in the world.

Hundreds of thousands have been won through their ministries.

Millions of dollars have been sent around the world to support missions.

Tens of thousands have been trained and sent out to serve the Lord.

The whole nation is a better place because of the church's ministries.

Blessed are Will and Martha, who died in the Lord, and their works are still following them, even though the investment was made one hundred years ago.

A smart Kindergarten kid will learn to use what God has placed in his hands, so he can keep working after graduation.

Your Opportunity To Invest Is Now

Now we have such a short time to labor. We have all of eternity to rest. You may ask, "What would my kids say if I sold their inheritance?"

Wait a minute right there! **Whose inheritance**? I thought it belonged to God and that He had placed you over it as a steward, to manage it for His interest and glory.

"Well, what would my kids say if I sold it and gave it to the Lord?"

Oh, they would probably be mad at you for a while. But at the Judgment Seat they will say, "Mom and Pop weren't so dumb after all. They sure made wise decisions and investments."

TIME IS RUNNING OUT

> But at the Judgment Seat they will say, "Mom and Pop weren't so dumb after all. They sure made wise decisions and investments."

If one hasn't understood this principle of laying up treasures in Heaven by investing in the 6 billion harvest of souls before he dies, then he will have missed his eternal opportunity.

Please visualize standing before our Lord of the harvest. Look into His pleading eyes and hear the pathos in His voice, "Why stand ye here all the day idle?" How will you answer this direct question?

He has given you everything! He has designed you to share in His eternal glory. You still have life, just as feeble old Abraham and Sarah had life. God blessed them at their point of willingness and faith, and they suddenly went from being barren and unfulfilled, to the "father of all nations."

What would a smart Kindergarten kid do?

POINTS TO PONDER

- A wise Kindergarten kid will **keep on working after graduation**.

- The Philippian church **invested** in Paul's ministry.

- One grain of corn becomes 300 stalks of corn.

- Invest in people **with the possibility of winning thousands** of souls after graduation.

- One keeps working after death by **making wise decisions** while still living.

LESSON SIX QUESTIONS
The Way To Keep Working After Kindergarten

MONDAY – THE WAY TO KEEP WORKING

1. The _____ teaches that although you _____ physically, you can _____ working even though your _____ is in the _____.

2. Paul won many _____ to Christ, and the _____ was _____ by God with _____ credit for their salvation.

3. From _____ grain of _____ comes _____ of thousands of ears of _____.

4. Although he is _____ (he graduated), he is _____ heard on over 1000 _____ stations _____ every day.

5. _____ time a soul is _____, portion of the credit goes to _____ accounts.

TUESDAY – HOW TO INVEST YOUR MONEY

1. Sometimes you worked while in _____, or when you were _____.

2. The _____ of giving in are that they have _____ their _____ to live and are just _____ to die.

3. You would be _____ to "_____ up _____" for yourself by investing in the _____ work.

4. You can _____ discomfort while _____ on a job in order to have _____ to invest in your _____ bank account.

5. Become a _____ role model of what a _____ is and how a Christian _____ in adverse conditions.

WEDNESDAY – A GREAT INVESTMENT IS IN INSTITUTIONS

1. When one finds a _____ principle concerning any _____ of life and _____ it, then he is _____ of success.

2. God moved on one man's _____ to transfer his physical _____ into _____, eternal _____.

3. The description of "_____ *it at the apostles feet*" *indicates that it was a* ____ *of* _____. (Acts 4:36-37)

4. _____ became one of the most _____ and _____ Christians in the whole Bible.

5. The eternal need that could be _____ if he was _____ to _____ his earthly assets into spiritual, _____ investments.

139

THURSDAY – A GREAT INVESTMENT

1. "_____ *are the dead which die in the Lord from henceforth: Yea, saith the* _____, *that they may* _____ *from the labours; and their* _____ *do follow them.*" (Revelations 14:13)

2. A _____ who _____ look up to, _____ to be in your place, or to _____ your blessing.

3. This _____ announcement is about God's _____ savings plan.

4. You _____ up there _____ in the Savior's love and your _____ are compounding on earth.

5. "*Well done, thou good and* _____ *servant: thou* _____ *been faithful over a* _____ *things, I will make thee* _____ *over many things: enter thou into the* _____ *of thy lord.*" (Matthew 25:21)

FRIDAY – A GIFT THAT HAS BEEN COMPOUNDING

1. God impressed upon their hearts to sell their beautiful little _____ and _____ the _____ to the building fund.

2. A _____ country church was _____ into one of the most mighty churches in _____ and in the _____.

140

3. "Mom and Pop _____ so _____ after all. They sure made _____ decisions and _____."

4. _____ into His _____ eyes and _____ the pathos in His _____, "_____ stand ye here all the day _____?"

5. They _____ went from being _____ and _____, to the "father of all nations."

DAILY DECLARATION

Repeat aloud each morning and evening:

"When I get to Heaven, I will find that the only money I saved was the money I gave."

MEMORY VERSE

For whosoever shall save his life shall lose it; but whosoever shall lose his life for my sake and the gospel's, the same shall save it." (Mark 8:25)

CHECK BLOCK AFTER REPEATING

	Mon.	Tues.	Wed.	Thurs	Fri.	Sat.	Sun.
A.M.							
P.M.							

I will strive to become a channel of blessing because Jesus said, *"It is more blessed to give than to receive."*

Signature

_____

EPILOGUE

*Is any thing too hard for the Lord?
At the time appointed I will return
unto thee, according to the time of
life, and Sarah shall have a son.*
(Genesis 18:14)

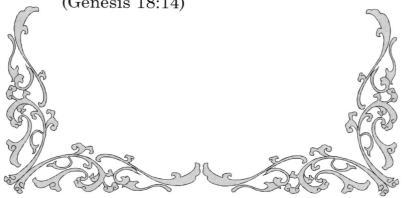

EPILOGUE

The Retirement of Father Abraham

WHAT IF ABRAHAM HAD RETIRED?

Let us imagine that Abram, when he became 65 years old, went into his tent where Sarah sat perspiring. The day before, they had experienced another sandstorm, and today the sun was blistering hot.

"I'm tired of all this waiting on God. I'm really tired of all this sand and heat. I think I have earned the right, after 65 years, to have a little relaxation and comfort," he said to Sarah.

"You are right, Abram. Besides, we could wait on God's promise over on the shores of the Mediterranean, where the sea breezes blow," encouraged his wife.

Thus Abram announced his retirement and they were soon living in a much better climate. By today's standards, Abram made a good decision. He would have fit right into this 21st generation crowd of 65 million Americans.

WHO IS ABRAM?

Someone questions, "Who is this Abram fellow? I have heard about Abraham, but not Abram. Who is he?"

> One man's retirement would have changed the world drastically and forever.

That is the point! If Abram had retired at 65 years of age, the world would have never heard of Abraham. God changed Abram's name to Abraham because he did not retire, but continued on in his effort to fulfill God's purpose for his life.

If he had retired at 65, there would not have been any Abraham, the father of the faithful. He would have been Abram, the father of one rebel son, Ishmael.

- There would have been no Isaac.

- There would have been no nation of Israel.

- There would have been no Christ-child.

- There would be no glorious 1000-year reign for Abram.

One man's retirement would have changed the world drastically and forever.

WHY ABRAHAM DID NOT RETIRE

God Spoke To Him

Abraham may have been like the millions of other men who lived on the earth during his lifetime if he hadn't talked to God. As he spoke to God, God spoke to him.

Faith cometh by hearing, and hearing by the word of God. (Romans 10:17)

God's First Promise To Abram In Haran

Now the Lord had said unto Abram, Get thee out of thy country, and from they kindred, and from the father's house, unto a land that I will shew thee: And I will make of thee a great nation, and I will bless thee, and make thy name great; and thou shalt be a blessing: And I will bless them that bless thee, and curse them that curseth thee: and in thee shall all families of the earth be blessed. (Genesis12:1-3)

God's Second Promise To Abram In Canaan

And the Lord said unto Abram, after that Lot was separated from him, Lift up now thine eyes, and look from the place where thou art northward, and southward, and eastward, and westward: For all the land which thou seest, to thee will I give it, and to thy seed for-ever. (Genesis 13:14-15)

God's Third Promise to Abraham in Hebron

And, behold, the word of the Lord came unto him, saying, This shall not be thine heir; but he that shall come forth out of thine own bowels shall be thine heir. And he brought him forth abroad, and said, Look now toward heaven, and tell the stars, if thou be able to number them: and he said unto him, So shall thy seed be. And he believed in the Lord; and he counted it to him for righteousness. (Genesis 15:4-6)

WHY YOU SHOULD NOT RETIRE

There are good reasons why you should not retire. Talk to God about it and then listen to His voice.

God Has Spoken to You

What? know ye not that your body is the temple of the Holy Ghost which is in you, which ye have of God, and ye are not your own? For ye are bought with a price: therefore glorify God in your body, and in your spirit, which are God's. (1 Corinthians 6:19-20)

God Has Spoken To You A Second Time

I beseech you therefore, brethren, by the mercies of God, that ye present your bodies a living sacrifice, holy, acceptable unto God, which is your reasonable service. And be not conformed to this world: but be ye transformed by the renewing of your mind, that ye may prove what is that good, and acceptable, and perfect, will of God." (Romans 12:1-2)

God Is Still Speaking To You

And about the eleventh hour he went out, and found others standing idle, and saith unto them, Why stand ye here all the day idle? They say unto him, Because no man hath hired us. He saith unto them, Go ye also into the vineyard; and whatsoever is right, that shall ye receive. (Matthew 20:6-7)

Prove what is that good, and acceptable, and perfect, will of God.

GOD BLESSES HIS CHILDREN IN THEIR OLD AGE

Remember, this world's greatest accomplishment were obtained by people after they reached the age of 60.

God Extended The Lives Of Abraham And Sarah

Abraham, at the age of 100, saw God work a miracle in his wife, Sarah, as he transformed her from an old woman back into a beautiful young woman who was able to give birth to Isaac.

149

This was one of God's greatest miracles and He performed it on two old people in order to accomplish His will and purpose in their lives.

> You, in the second semester of The Kindergarten Phase of Eternity, are still alive. Your work is not finished.

God Is Not a Respecter of Persons

God longs to bless you in your old age, and He is not a respecter of persons. He could extend your life. He could perform a miracle in your life so you can do great and mighty things for Him.

HUNDREDS OF YEARS LATER

Hundreds of years after old Abraham and his wife, Sarah, believed God, refused to retire, the world is still talking about them in admiration and wonderment. This respect and honor will continue on throughout the ages to come.

God is still asking, *"Why stand ye here all the day idle,"* while the masses are perishing?

You, in the second semester of *the Kindergarten Phase of Eternity*, are still alive. Your work is not finished. You still have an opportunity to do something that may have people talking in wonderment and admiration hundreds of years after your graduation.

Remember, all things are possible.

Who knows what you and God can accomplish if you only refuse to quit and obey Him?

ANSWER KEY

"For we must all appear before the judgment seat of Christ; that every one may receive the things done in his body, according to that he hath done, whether it be good or bad."

(2 Corinthians 5:10)

LESSON ONE
Kindergarten Is Important

MONDAY

1. concern – eternal
2. very – overall
3. lifetime
4. hindrance – parents – wisely

TUESDAY

1. misspent – hinder – millennium – eternal
2. natural
3. directly – forever
4. one – earth – tick – Heaven
5. rests – service – 1000 year – eternal

WEDNESDAY

1. thinking – one – philosophy
2. question – you
3. created – marvelous – inhabit
4. position – stewardship
5. what – purpose – talents

THURSDAY

1. lighteth – man
2. Jesus – live – being
3. created – pleasure – created
4. surprised – recognize
5. body – spirit – God's

FRIDAY

1. not – own – created – life
2. creative – one – ownership
3. elevate – royalty – 1000 year
4. have – legally
5. desire – share – glory

LESSON TWO

The Development of Talent in Kindergarten

MONDAY

1. structured – objectives – phase
2. God – God – God – God's
3. God – himself – life
4. infinite – image – created – world – eternal
5. something – please share

TUESDAY

1. devil – deception – thievery
2. hurt – harm – dying – lesson plans

3. came – life – victorious
4. Christian – good – acceptable – perfect
5. life – glory – happiness

WEDNESDAY

1. loving – teacher – Kindergarten
2. eternal
3. troubles – encounter – overcome – designed – glory
4. light – moment – eternity

THURSDAY

1. body – follow – do
2. in – of
3. study – approved
4. not – world
5. renews – Bible – following – pleasing
6. obeys – attributes – closer – joy

FRIDAY

1. allows – own
2. not – ought
3. submit – thing
4. humble – submissive – free – bless
5. vigilant – watching – self-sufficient

LESSON THREE

The Place to Prepare for Living Is Kindergarten

MONDAY

1. people – lives – discover
2. you – Kindergarten – struggles – days
3. difficulties – eternal
4. pictures – papa
5. learn – observation

TUESDAY

1. myself – finish – course
2. out – purpose – life
3. fruit – he – winneth – wise
4. Daniel – super
5. learn – wise – souls

WEDNESDAY

1. why – important – see – important
2. man – seek – save
3. go – Heaven – change
4. home – tell – thee
5. examples – example – seeking

THURSDAY

1. all – preach – every
2. Father – me – you

3. billion – Lord's – perishing
4. children – idle – children – hell
5. screaming – black – pain – hope

FRIDAY

1. eleventh – emergency
2. emergency – army – workers – vineyard
3. amnesty – failures – mistakes – condition – my
4. forget – answering – call – greatest
5. hire – respond – emergency

LESSON FOUR

The Basic Lessons to Be Learned in Kindergarten

MONDAY

1. Kindergarten – graduation – life – graduation
2. better – day – birth
3. spend – time – physical – this
4. viewed – shadow – races – gone
5. puff

TUESDAY

1. profit – gain – wealthy – soul – misspends
2. learn – save – body
3. praying – glorify – want
4. develop – would – this
5. learn – obey – please

WEDNESDAY

1. persistent – asking – seeking – petition
2. His – level – discipline – mentoring
3. learn – impulses – no
4. listen – tells – do
5. position – stewardship

THURSDAY

1. not – earth
2. must – treasures – Heaven – emphatic
3. good – acceptable – includes –
   earthly – eternal
4. All – world – burned
5. generation – give – tithe

FRIDAY

1. goeth – warfare – charges
2. understand – all – time – energy – spiritual
3. so – Lord – live
4. gave – 100% - lay – themselves – investing
5. father – more – child – Father

LESSON FIVE

An Advanced Lesson To Be Learned For Leadership

MONDAY

1. kids – well – excel

2. beings – nature
3. thing – earth – gave
4. leader – grow – grace
5. grow – grace – knowledge

TUESDAY

1. command – led – faith
2. learned – 10 – percentage – each
3. way – grow – lay – Heaven
4. little – little – have – little
5. Sow – reap

WEDNESDAY

1. obeys – he – not – all
2. smart – studies – enjoy
3. find – use – happy
4. end – described – piercing – sorrows
5. only – wealth – That – me

THURSDAY

1. sore – seen – riches – hurt
2. laboured – wind – naked – naked
3. parents – riches – live – be
4. assume – better
5. use – money – bring

FRIDAY

1. beautiful – wanted – enjoy – wealth
2. way – enjoy – increase

3. gives – use – blessing – Lord's
4. giving – work – unbelievable – everlasting
5. look – short – life – transpire

LESSON SIX

The Way To Keep Working After Kindergarten

MONDAY

1. Bible – die – keep – body – grave
2. souls – church – rewarded – partial
3. one – corn – tens – corn
4. dead – still – radio – worldwide
5. every – saved – their

TUESDAY

1. pain – sick
2. results – lost – purpose – waiting
3. working – lay – treasures – Lord's
4. suffer – working – money – eternal
5. good – Christian – acts

WEDNESDAY

1. Biblical – facet – follows – assured
2. heart – assets – spiritual – dividends
3. laid – lot – money
4. Barnabas – honored – respected
5. filled – willing – transfer – eternal

THURSDAY

1. Blessed – Spirit – rest – works
2. person – people – desiring – receive
3. unbelievable – greatest
4. are – basking – works
5. faithful – hast – few – things – ruler – joy

FRIDAY

1. home – give – money
2. little – transformed – America – world
3. weren't – dumb – wise – investments
4. look – pleading – hear – voice –
   why – idle
5. suddenly – barren – unfulfilled

FROM THE AUTHOR

The Back To Basics Follow-Up, Protection and Development, and Rehabilitation programs are based upon the teachings found in the pastoral commission as given to Peter by Jesus in John 21:15-17. Jesus very emphatically spelled out Peter's responsibilities as pastor in three separate charges.

1. *"Feed My Lambs,"* – or literally stated, "pacify my babies."

2. *"Feed My Sheep,"* – the ones who are weak, sick or lame.

3. "Feed My Sheep," – the strong, healthy, prime, fruitful sheep.

These **charges to the first pastor teach the methodology** of feeding, as well as the **responsibility for feeding**. It also teaches the way an infant learns – by observing the example set before him.

The pastor, as tender nurse (1 Thess. 2:7) or spiritual father (1 Thess. 2:11), sets the proper role model before God's family and trains the members of the church by his example (**holy, just and blameless** [1 Thess. 2:10], and **exhorting, comforting and charging** [1 Thess. 2:11]). He trains them until they have made the transition from defenseless babes to fully grown, working saints.

He trains the older members of his church to become role models (pastor's assistants): taking the milk of the Word to the new converts and **pacifying** them (loving, protecting and giving them security)until they are able to walk alone and are secure in the church family.

NEW CONVERTS CARE DISCIPLESHIP PROGRAM

The Follow-Up Phase: As soon as a person is born-again, he needs to have the shield of faith put on him. This is done by giving him a new birth certificate and teaching him seven principles that will protect and help him grow (found in the *Salvation to Serve* booklet).

Salvation To Service booklet
Questions Concerning Baptism
Four Transformational Truths (4-week study)

The Protection and Development Phase: A spiritual role model is appointed over the new convert as an extension of the pastor's ministry for three to six months. By living in a just and unblamable way, the role model sets a good example for the new convert. He also goes through the *Milk of the Word* with the new convert, helping him learn how to rightly divide the Word (in other words, feed himself) until he can study alone.

Milk of the Word (10-week study)
Mission of the Church (12-week study)
Meat of the Word (10-week study)

The Rehabilitation Phase: The statement Jesus made to the first pastor, "Feed My Sheep," (wounded and hurting) teaches that there is a need in many Christian lives for rehabilitation. Something in their lives has completely stopped them from growing, or is restricting their spiritual growth in some way. They hae been wounded or offended and have retreated within themselves. They desperately need the information found in these lessons, loving encouragemnt and rehabilitation.

Helping Hands For Hurting People (4-week study)

BOOKS FOR SOUL-WINNING TRAINING

Essentials For Successful Soul-Winning
Foreknowledge in the Light Of Soul-Winning
Designed To Win

New Testament Ministries
Dr. James Wilkins
1700 Beaver Creek Dr.
Powell, TN 37849
817-909-8010
865-938-8182

CD AND DVD PRICE LIST

Drama At The Cross – CD and DVD $10.00
A Final Flight To Heaven – CD and DVD $10.00

SOUL-WINNING TRAINING SERIES

Green Beans and the Power of the Gospel $10.00
    DVD featuring soul-winning principles
    and soul-winning presentations

The Countdown Method $20.00
    Album of 3 CD's featuring:
        5 Approach Questions
        4 Spiritual Principles
        3 Possibilities At The Cross
        2 By 2 For Best Results
        1 Supreme Purpose
        Learn To Work With The Holy Spirit

THE MILLENNIAL KINGDOM SERIES
        $10.00 each or $30.00 for set

Thy Kingdom Come – CD and DVD
Curing the Carnal Corinthians – DVD
The Call To the 11th Hour Harvest – DVD
Who Are These Kings? – CD and DVD

Churches: Please contact **New Testament Ministries** for quantity prices.

For a complete listing of the author's books, please visit us at:

Website: www.jameswilkins.org
or contact us at:
Email: pwilkins96@sbcglobal.net

YAKIMA BIBLE BAPTIST CHURCH
6201 TIETON DRIVE
YAKIMA, WA. 98908
509-966-1912